# MAGIC HANDS

## PROFESSIONAL
## CARD TRICK
## SECRETS REVEALED

D0814240

# MAGIC HANDS

## PROFESSIONAL CARD TRICK SECRETS REVEALED

# HERBERT L. BECKER

PLAIN SIGHT
PUBLISHING

An imprint of Cedar Fort, Inc.
Springville, Utah

© 2017 Herbert L. Becker

ISBN 13: 978-1-4621-2059-8

Published by Plain Sight Publishing, an imprint of Cedar Fort, Inc.
2373 W. 700 S., Springville, UT 84663
Distributed by Cedar Fort, Inc., www.cedarfort.com

LIBRARY OF CONGRESS CATALOGING-IN-PUBLICATION DATA ON FILE

Cover design by Priscilla Chaves
Cover design © 2017 by Cedar Fort, Inc.
Edited and typeset by Casey Nealon and Jessica Romrell

Printed in the United States of America

10  9  8  7  6  5  4  3  2  1

Printed on acid-free paper

*Marjie, thank you for your inspiration and encouragement.*

*Ted Shistle Jr. for your fabulous photos throughout this work and your nearly fifty years of friendship.*

*Nechemiah and Ezra for your early readings and experimentation of the tricks.*

*Dovid for keeping the magic alive.*

# CONTENTS

# CONTENTS

# OTHER BOOKS BY HERBERT L BECKER

All The Secrets of Magic Revealed-Lifetime Books 1995

More Magic Secrets-Magic Web Publishing 1997

Magic Secrets the CD Rom-Magic Web Publishing 1998

101 Greatest Magic Secrets Revealed-Citadel Press 2002

The Magic Secrets of David Blaine: The street magician revealed-Lifetime Books 2007

# ACKNOWLEDGMENTS

I'm happy to say that this book truly took on a life of its own and practically wrote itself. I had the good fortune to be the conductor who brought all the bits and pieces together. I was truly inspired by Outliers, the work of Malcolm Gladwell. It was reading his wonderful book that set the flywheel in motion for my own work. I have since been in touch with Mr. Gladwell and his comments have been an inspiration to me.

I leaned heavily on others for insight, inspiration, facts, figures, and quotes. This book is much better because of them. I thank Louisa Dalton for insights into the math genius of Stanford, Dr. Persi Diaconis. I thank Steve Wozniak, cofounder of Apple Computers and a fan of magic, who had an early read of the manuscript and whose insights and friendship I am so privileged to have.

I give special thanks to my son Nechemiah Becker, who worked with me on the manuscript to ensure that the tricks worked and the instructions were clear enough for a twelve-year-old (which is how old he happened to be at the time) to follow and understand.

Thank you Wikipedia for various references and fact checking. Thank you statistical expert Surajit Basu for insights into shuffling a deck of cards.

My longtime friendship and collaborations with the late Walter Gibson and Burling "Volta" Hull continue to be inspirational to me. I am certain that their words live on in me and in all my works. Walter and I were introduced and put together by the late David Boehm, owner and publisher of Sterling Books. Walter and I worked together on several books. Some were published, and others never did see their way into print. Nevertheless, it was never boring working with the great man. We'd meet often at the Sterling Publishing offices and other times at the Algonquin Hotel, both in New York City.

My other mentor, Burling Hull, was in his twilight years living in nearby DeLand, Florida, when we met, and I still cherish our time together. It is said that Burling Hull wrote more books, pamphlets, and articles on the subject of magic than anyone else. Burling also ghostwrote books for others including Harry Houdini. I'd visit Burling whenever I was in town and would normally find him in his home office surrounded by his books. Even after he was legally blind and could no longer use his typewriter (you younger folks can look up that item on the Internet), he would dictate into a recorder for his part-time assistant to type his books out for him. Until the very end, Burling loved magic and writing about it.

Thanks to Stanford mathematician Dr. Persi Diaconis, who used to say, "When somebody says they're going to do a math-magic trick, it sounds as if they're going to deal cards in piles, and you'll all fall asleep. I try to develop tricks that are good tricks that don't look like math, but that have real math hidden in them."[1]

And a special thanks to my son Dovid Becker for your encouragement and help. Now if I could only find the magic trick that would encourage you to clean your room. Dovid is a certified firefighter and uses skills, not magic, as a first responder.

---

1        "Math and Magic Equal Sum Fun," Inside Magic, April 20, 2006, accessed January 25, 2017, http://www.insidemagic.com/magicnews/2006/04/math-and-magic-equal-sum-fun.

# INTRODUCTION

## Completing 10,000 hours of practice means everything, but how did the magician get the rabbit in there in the first place?

Congratulations! In your hand you are holding a book that contains card tricks and magic performance advice that is not available anywhere else to the general public. These are secrets which are guarded by the world's greatest magic performers who learned this information from their mentors or from books sold only to magicians. The tricks are those you will see presented by the greatest of magicians on stage and on television. Don't let the tricks fool you with some of their seemingly simplistic instructions because knowing how the mechanics of the trick work is only a small part of knowing how to perform the trick for others.

Read the tricks, practice the tricks, and create a rhythm and banter for your presentation. Start by reading the entire book and make sure you have a good deck of cards with you while you read. After you read the book, certain tricks will seem to talk to you. Maybe you've seen the trick performed by a magical superstar or maybe the trick just seems to encompass your personality. Whatever it is, zero in on that trick and begin the long journey toward making it your own.

Magic tricks with cards is a wonderful way to begin the process of becoming a prestidigitator no matter what your end goals might be. This is the start of that road map. It all lies before you.

Magic has been around for a very long time and I don't see it going away anytime soon.

The wonders of magic and the wonders of life have a great deal in common. Both are a mystery to the general public and neither can be easily understood. Regardless of how closely you watch the magician, he still fools you. No matter how closely you watch the news on TV, something is still going to surprise you. No matter how often you see a butterfly flutter by, you are still dazzled by its beauty—at least I am.

Magic is truly the simple idea of the performer knowing the secret and the audience not so much. When a comedian tells a joke, they might take you in one direction only to surprise you with the punch line. If you knew the punch line before the joke was told, it might not be as funny and certainly not as surprising.

Just as with a comedian, it comes down to timing. It takes great timing for a joke to be told and great timing to fool people with a trick. Have you ever tried telling a joke that made you laugh when you heard it, only to see it fall flat when you try to tell it yourself? It's all about the delivery and the presentation. Here is where it all begins for you, regardless if this is your first book on magic or if you have been studying and practicing magic for many years. For the first time, you will come face-to-face with professional card tricks in a presentation that anyone will be able to follow.

Recently, I planted a garden in my yard for the first time. I planted seeds, seedlings, and small plants. I watered and nourished them and, to my delight and wonder, they began to grow. A once dark corner of my yard eventually exploded into a rainbow of colors and scents. Soon came birds, bees, and the aforementioned butterflies. It was truly magical and a wonderful change to my yard. Even though I thought I knew what to expect, the end result was no less beautiful and was a bit surprising because I did not know what I was capable of doing.

This has a great deal in common with performing magic. You can read and practice a trick in this book and it might seem simple or not so magical to you after you have performed it for yourself in front of a mirror dozens of times. Then one day you perform the trick for someone else and you watch the astonishment in their face when you fool them. It will be at that moment when you will understand what magic is all about. It is the wonderment and surprise that others will receive when you fool them—and those feelings are priceless.

If you are expecting a book on magic tricks, or better yet, magic secrets, well, this is it . . . sort of. If you are looking for the wisdom of the ages and how to maintain a healthier outlook on life, well, that is what you have in your hands. Magic and the magic tricks you will learn in this book can be used as a metaphor for life in general. Life itself is magic; we come into this world an empty slate and then we grow, mature, and become experts at being us. Here you will read a trick for the first time; practice it and you can also become an expert at it. As your knowledge of the mechanics of the tricks grows, you will also grow in confidence and style.

A side benefit of learning tricks and how to perform them in front of others is the confidence to talk to groups of people. I always considered myself a shy person and the confidence I gained with magic helped me to become a better person in all aspects of my life, especially when it came to speaking to others. My lifelong pal, John Poalucci, would tell me that the only reason I was popular with the girls when I was a teenager was my ability to perform magic tricks. That was partly true, because performing gave me a reason to talk to people. Asking someone if they'd like to see a trick is always an easy way to break the ice and begin the conversation. As a business leader, I've always called upon my ability to stand before a group of people and keep them attentive—all of this because I decided to learn a card trick one day.

I have written a great deal about magic and the media has written a great deal about me and what I have written, and somewhere along the way, it seemed that there was more to life than magic, secrets, and lawsuits.

For the most part, it's fun to fool people—not in a cruel way, but in a happy way for me. I enjoy watching the faces of people I fool while per-forming magic. As I weave the trick along with a story, I watch their faces and their eyes. Sometimes I can almost hear what they are thinking when I use misdirection and then, when I complete the trick, it is the sense of awe and surprise on their face that gives me such joy and gratification.

There is an underlying misconception that people enjoy being fooled. They do not; at least, I don't like it and I have yet to find someone who tells me that they like it. What people seem to enjoy is trying to figure things out and, if they cannot get the answer on their own, they like to find the answer. Magic might be the example, but society as a whole has been seeking answers to everything since the dawn of man. Why else would Columbus sail across the ocean or Galileo Galilei search the stars? They and many more did it to find answers. We continue our search and many of us use Google for our own personal search.

From our search, we will begin to understand how and why magic tricks work, both from the point of view of the magician and from the point of view of the audience.

You do not need to be a professional magician to want to perform and you do not need to be a magician to know how magic works!

There are many magic trick books written for professional magicians and many more written for amateur magicians. Until now, trying to find a book of professional level magic tricks, which are available for the amateur, has been unheard of. Professional level magic books are not available in the bookstore chains or libraries, but reserved for the professional magician at the best magic shops and at premium prices.

In this book, I have dipped into the treasure box of the professional magician and come up with many card tricks that anyone at any level will be able to learn and perform just like the pros. Some of the tricks might seem easy to the reader, but the tricks are always easy to understand once you know the secret. In most of these tricks, you don't tell those watching how the trick will end, instead, you bring them on a magical journey as the trick unfolds and the ending is surprising to those watching the performance.

These are professional tricks whose secrets have been guarded, and until now, only available to those who are considered professional magicians. You don't need to be a professional magician to perform the tricks in this book you only need the desire to be a performer.

In this book, you will enter the world that is dominated by David Blaine, Harry Houdini, Criss Angel, and the rest of the secretive world of the professional magician.

I heard a story what went like this:

"I know three hundred card tricks. How many do you know?" the teenager asked the professional magician.

The magician looked at the youth quizzically. "I should say," the magician responded dryly, "that I know about eight."

The magician was making a point with which all professional magicians are familiar. To perform card tricks entertainingly, you must not only know how the tricks are done, but how to do them well. If you only realize success in one or two tricks from this book, that might be enough for you, especially if you perform them well. In fact, unless it is your desire to become a professional magician, learning a couple of tricks from this book will be enough to succeed.

Some tricks you will learn in this book might seem more natural for you or more to your liking or personal style. Learn the tricks you like the most and practice them often. Make them your own and over time, these tricks will be similar to a joke told by a great comedian. You will have the timing down, but you may not know what to expect from those watching you.

There is a vast difference between the two; one need only watch the same card tricks performed by a novice and by an expert card conjurer to see it. The novice knows the mechanics of so many card tricks that he cannot do any one feat really well, whereas the professional performs a smaller number of card tricks, but knows how to create the best possible impression upon those who watch. After reading this book and practicing, the amateur will be as good as the pro.

# CHAPTER ONE

## A Glimpse into the History of Magic

Magic is an antediluvian art. As Sherman Ripley observed in his classic book, *An Introduction to Magic*: "It precedes written history and is probably simultaneous with the beginning of folklore. Ancient priests and medicine men practiced crude forms of magic. This is paralleled today in the incantations and taboos of the medicine men of primitive tribes still inhabiting remote islands or living in the depths of jungles."[1]

Our fancy of this legend has been the foundation of countless books and movies, regardless if the author sets the story in historic or futuristic times. The success of the Harry Potter series is a testament to this process. Harry Potter, the boy wizard, has the powers so many of us wish we had and allows us to enter his world of enchantment and prestidigitation. The romance of magic is simply too hard to resist.

Those from the older generation remember a television show called *Bewitched*, in which a young housewife can wiggle her nose and make magic happen, all to the chagrin of her non-magical husband. The show was a great success and people all over the world tried to wiggle their nose and create miracles.

Why do we love watching magic? We know that we are being tricked, but we love the challenge. However, I digress. As we know today, civilization started as people began to group together and as those groups burgeoned and grew, we went from individuals to communities. So much

---

1    Sherman Ripley, *An Introduction to Magic: 141 Professional Tricks you can do with Coins, Cards, Silks and Billiard Balls—Secrets of Famous Stage Tricks* (Blumenfeld Press, 2013).

was unknown. Was the world flat? It certainly looked that way. What caused the thunder, what caused the wind, what brought the rain? Filling this gap were those who were called priests, astrologers, soothsayers, and magicians.

As these people of wonder continued to expand in importance, they quickly became those closest to the seats of power. Royalty, leaders, and tyrants all wanted these keen people to advise them, predict the future, and ask for success and riches from the mysterious powers that seemed to rule the lands. All of a sudden, the magician was the power behind the throne.

For the most part, the communities emerged as isolated populations with little or no interactions with others outside their own territory. To that end, cultures that experienced similar environmental and natural phenomena each found their own ways of explaining our world to their own people.

To me, Oriental magic is filled with folklore and legends. Living near the sea created the stories of dragons, rainbows, and snowcapped mountains. It is a more traditional style of magic. Their magic was often performed to the sounds of simple musical instruments such as chimes, bells, and cymbals. To this day, this style of magic continues to enthrall audiences. Wind was an important element to Oriental magic and the chimes seemed to mimic the sound waves created by wind. The Oriental magic also used primitive smoke bombs and firecrackers during their magic shows.

Greece and the Italian peninsula was much more profound in magic and its mystery. Countries of great sailors and their lore permeated their traditions of magic as well as worship. Instead of telling stories of dragons like the Orient, they believed in a world that was flat enough to fall off the edge of an ocean. Instead of dragons, they feared sea monsters.

Storytellers would tell great tales of sea monsters and because of the fear and unknown, the sailors would request magical items to bring aboard the ship which could protect them and ward off evils. The magicians were in high demand and would in turn be able to demand great treasures in order to protect the sailors and the ships they sailed with.

Greek magicians would use masks and costumes to perform their magic. They had huge theatrical sets often using the setting of the sea as the background. It was not unheard of to produce a huge sea monster and use it to strike fear into their audience.

A great wizard of a royal court or a high priest to the ruling party would be the ones who would prophesy, read the stars, or predict the future. To the ones in control, starting a war or when to sail a ship would be a moment of reflection and a certain consultation of the wise wizard.

The awesome empires of Egypt and their hot desert lands could only survive with the Nile River. Rain was rare and the Pharaoh would employ many magicians who would call upon all their magic in order to please their deities and bring rain. The biblical story of Joseph rising to power came at a time when a great drought was on the horizon based upon the Pharaoh's dreams. Joseph was smarter than the court magicians and was able to interpret the dreams. His plans for the future and how to survive the onslaught of famine proved so successful that Joseph became the head of the royal court and was considered by the Pharaoh as the greatest magician in all the land.

No empire would be complete without a solid group of magicians to guide, read horoscopes, and explain why a summer was too hot or a winter too cold.

Perhaps you have heard of King Arthur, the immortalized king of Britain and his Round Table of brave knights. We know all about him, right? Well, my research revealed to me that Arthur was definitively Welsh, Celtic, or Breton. He fought the Saxons in the north, in the south, or in Wales, around the year 450, 500, or 525. He may or may not have been a king, who was or was not named Arthur. Some say he was a figure of imagination while others insist he was a real person. This leaves this subject as clear as mud.

Certainly, he was a man of myth and legend, and just as famous was his court magician Merlin.

Merlin was a man of magic as well as great wisdom. He could cast spells with an eye of newt and a wave of his hand. An incantation and a little hocus pocus later, some sort of magic would occur. But just as we know little of King Arthur, we truly know nothing more about Merlin. Legends of sea monsters and legends of people like Merlin stay with us because we love them and we wish them to be true.

About magicians in this time period, Ripley said, "These magi of the Dark Ages were a mixture of astrologer, faker, chemist and fortune-teller.

They sold nostrums, charms, love-potions and for an extra consideration – poisons."[2]

One of these successful fraudsters was named Cagliostro, a mischievous man who was disowned by his family early on after he was expelled from a monastery school for misconduct. He managed to travel the world before settling in Malta as a man of magic.

After establishing himself in Malta, he continued to travel the world, selling many different alchemistic elixirs and powders. Along the way, he became associated with a new group calling themselves freemasons. He eventually died in prison in 1795.[2]

In the Middle East, the rise of the Torah and later the Bible brought a combination of magic, monotheism, and a single devotion of the Hebrew people. For the most part, the Hebrew people had a landlocked, desert, and nomad community. Living separately from the other communities who might have had hundreds of gods and beliefs, the Hebrews believed in one god, and this god was the only one who would have the power to change the world.

As the Jewish, Christian, and Muslim beliefs grew and began to take hold of the Near and Middle East, great thinkers began to read all that was available about God and his world. These deep thinkers and learned men would begin to piece together what they believed to be the creation and how the world survived from day to day.

As people began to further explore and civilize the world, great schools and academies of religious learning were opening and people were learning more of the seemingly magical world around them. Many learned men would travel and preach the words of God and His wondrous creations. Now magic was taking on a different feel. Planting a seed would produce a tree. Even a small seed would produce a humongous tree. This was the greatest magic of all and people, not just magicians, would be able to perform this magic. Can you imagine the first time a simple man planted a small seed and would watch it grow into a mighty cedar tree? At first it was a wonder but as time went on, it became common and the magic dissolved into a normal stream of life.

One of the most brilliant scholars of the time, Rambam, is known to this day. His birth name was Moses Maimonides and he was born on

<hr />

2    Hugh Chisholm, "Cagliostro, Alessandro, Count," *Encyclopedia Britannica*, volume 4 (Encyclopedia Britannica Company, 1910), 946.

March 30, 1135 in Córdoba, Spain.[3] He was a rabbi, physician, and philosopher. He traveled and lived in Morocco, Israel, and Egypt during the Middle Ages. He is called Rambam because it is an acronym of his name: Rabbi Moses ben Maimon.[4]

As one of the important medieval Hebrew philosophers of his time, he was influential to the Jews as well as to the gentiles. After gaining notoriety as a practicing physician, Rambam was appointed as a personal physician to Saladin, the sultan of Egypt. As a great writer, Rambam wrote copious works and books on Jewish law, which to this day is learned and studied by those of the Jewish faith.[4]

Civilization continued to march forward and there became a great divide between the "haves" and the "have nots." The wealthy owned vast lands and would have local populations of the poor till the land. The rich people were educated and knowledgeable for their time while the poor were kept away from any sort of education. The poor became fearful of what they did not know. Overlords used this fear to control their workforce by employing magicians to stir up the folklore of evil.

To fill this gap between the rich and the poor, the learned and the uneducated, came the clergy. They were able to easily, for the most part, stream between the groups. The clergy became the calming voice when the people had good times and bad, wars and slavery, labor and authority. As the interpreters of the Divine Spirit, these enlightened men were nothing more than the same magicians of old moving into a void created by the separation of cultures. These new men of magic were the burning torch of wisdom and contentment for the masses and they used their wizardry to befuddle and mystify the simple folks into believing that, for the most part, their flocks were who they were because of a mystical plan. A rock was a rock and could be no more than a rock whereas a caterpillar would change into a butterfly. Knowing this kept an order and the world continued to move forward. It must have been sad to have been a rock.

---

3      Ben Zion Bokser, "Moses Maimonides," *Encyclopedia Britannica*, last modified May 11, 2016, accessed January 25, 2017, https://www.britannica.com/biography/Moses-Maimonides.

4      Joseph Telushkin, "Moses Maimonides (Rambam)," Jewish Virtual Library, accessed January 25, 2017, http://www.jewishvirtuallibrary.org/moses-maimonides-rambam.

As for the magician, he continued to perform "miracles" and he never truly went away because he filled that need, that gap between what we see when we look up into the sky and ask why and the reality of everyday life.

The modern magician, it would seem to me, is a far cry from the wizards of old. Today, few believe that you will fall off the edge of the world and most can find answers to our questions by surfing on the Internet. The modern magician won't try to convince you of special powers or potions. He will tell you straight up that his is a world of trickery and perhaps a little bit of his hand being faster than your eye. He will challenge you and he will delight you and in the end you will leave with a sense of awe and then you move on to your smart phone to see the latest news and sports scores.

Perhaps that is why magic will always be popular. Walter Gibson, author of *The Shadow* and himself a magician as well as a mentor and friend to me, said it best when he told me that no one likes paying magicians, but just about everyone likes watching magic.

# Where to Start

Do not expect to become a finished artist overnight. It is safer not to saw a person in half at your first presentation. Beginners often try to present tricks before fully mastering them. My young sons love magic and when they learn a new trick, I can see myself in them. They read the instructions to the new trick and run to show it off. "Practice in front of a mirror first," I tell them. However, the excitement of the new trick is often too much for them. They want to rush to me to show me their modern miracle. It is better to be sure of the trick, the talk, and the routine before you present an effect.

The secrets of success are study and practice. For magicians, practice before a mirror is most important. Observing yourself from all angles, you see just how to stand, how to hold your arms, and how to make the best impression with your skills. The greatest magicians spent long practice periods before mirrors, scrutinizing every move before the presentation of an effect.

Misdirection is the magician's best colleague. Have you heard that the hand is quicker than the eye? This is certainly not true, but the adage has its foundation in magic. The magician makes his audience look in the wrong place. This is known as misdirection.

Here are Ripley's practical rules of misdirection:

The audience will look where you look.

The audience will look at anything that moves.

The audience will look at anything to which you point.

The audience will look toward a flash or light, a loud noise, a stumble or fall, a seeming accident.[5]

Hold out your hand, close your fist and stare at it, and those watching will follow suit. Wiggle a finger, shake your fist or move it while your other hand points to it and you will really have your audience curious about what might be held in your hand. Toss an imaginary item into the air and follow it with your eyes and your head, so too will your audience. It is simple and we have done this our entire life. Anyone who has entertained a young child while watching over them will know that we do all sorts of things to make the child smile or make them stop crying. We will make noises, sing, clap our hands, and make small toys dance before their eyes. We are trying to misdirect them from one thing onto another.

Have you ever grabbed off the nose of a baby and watched as they follow your hand, which they believe has their nose in it? Did you swallow that nose, make it pop out your cheek, and then place it safely back on the child's face? If you have, then you were doing the same magical misdirection that Houdini or mystical Merlin might have done when they performed their own tricks.

When you fooled the child you had your reasons; it might have just been to make them smile. The magician has their own reason; it is to entertain you and perhaps make you smile too.

---

5     Sherman Ripley, *An Introduction to Magic: 141 Professional Tricks you can do with Coins, Cards, Silks and Billiard Balls—Secrets of Famous Stage Tricks* (Blumenfeld Press, 2013).

# Magic with Cards—The Philosophy

Magic tricks will amaze and amuse your audience. And it can be an audience as small as a single person, on a stage as grand as Radio City Music Hall, or on television. Cards are the magician's easiest tools to use in performance.

First, it is easy to carry a deck of cards around with you; it is also easy to carry more than one deck. It is easier than carrying around just about any other magic apparatus.

With a deck of cards, you are ready to perform under just about any condition and in just about any situation. Even a borrowed deck of cards can be used to perform most of the tricks in this book.

Secondly, most everyone has seen a deck of cards and they are familiar with the different cards in a deck.

Third, a deck of cards is a rather ordinary item, almost considered a household item and the more ordinary the item you perform with, the more off guard your audience is.

Card magic is the illusion of magic using a deck of playing cards. Card magic is commonplace in magic performances, especially in close-up magic or parlor magic and street magic.

Playing cards became popular with magicians in the last century or so as they were props that were inexpensive, versatile, and easily manipulated. Although magicians have created and presented myriad illusions with cards, these illusions are generally considered to be built upon a few basic principles and techniques. Presentation and what the magician will say, called patter, during his act account for many of the variations.

Some card tricks have found their way into deception of another kind. A game called Three Card Monte has been used by shysters to cheat people out of money. In the game, three cards are used, normally two face cards and an ace. The trickster will mix the three cards on a table and tell you to watch carefully as the cards are mixed and to keep your eye on the ace. All cards are facedown until the shyster picks them up and shows all three. Then they are turned facedown and mixed. At first the unsuspecting victim can easily keep their eye on which card is the ace. Betting and winning starts to go south when the card man uses trickery to deceive the onlooker and win all of his money.

Card magic, in one form or another, likely dates from the time playing cards became commonly known, which is toward the second half of the fourteenth century. Over the past fifty-five years of working with cards, I have learned that as cards themselves evolved, so has the ability to use them for more than the card games they were created to play. As magic tools, using cards can be one of the best magic acts of them all.

# Card Magic Statistically Speaking

Persi Diaconis, professor of mathematics and statistics at Stanford, will often perform a card trick at meetings.[6] Having left his New York City home at fourteen to travel with a sleight-of-hand magician named Dai Vernon, the high-school dropout spent the next decade honing his skills in magic.[7]

By the time he was twenty-four years old, Persi had invented two card tricks using mathematics. A few years later, he began studying statistics at Harvard University.[7]

Persi considers his magician's tricks as tools for solving scientific dilemmas. In the book *A Lifetime of Puzzles* about mathematics writer Martin Gardner, he is quoted as saying:

> The way I do magic is very similar to mathematics. Inventing a magic trick and inventing a theorem are very, very similar activities in the following sense. In both subjects, you have a problem you're trying to solve with constraints. One difference between magic and mathematics is the competition. The competition in mathematics is a lot stiffer than in magic.[8]

---

6     Mark Shwartz, "Card tricks and mathematics: applying the magician's trade to numerical dilemmas," *Stanford News Service*, February 16, 2001, accessed January 5, 2017, https://web.stanford.edu/dept/news/pr/01/aaasdiaconis221.html.

7     Erica Klarreich, "For Persi Diaconis' Next Magic Trick," *Quanta Magazine*, April 14, 2015, accessed January 25, 2017, https://www.quantamagazine.org/20150414-for-persi-diaconis-next-magic-trick.

8     Edited by Erik D. Demaine, Martin L. Demaine, Tom Rodgers, A Lifetime of Puzzles: Honoring Marvin Gardner (Boca Raton: Taylor & Francis Group,

Statistically, if a man sits and shuffles a deck of fifty-two playing cards over and over, what happens? He shuffles quickly; he mixes the cards into a random order once per second.

A "repeat" happens when the order of the fifty-two cards in a shuffled deck is identical to the order of the fifty-two cards after any previous shuffle.

The man wants to shuffle until there is a 75% chance that he has dealt a repeat. How long will he be shuffling cards? How many combinations/ orders are there?

Well, the first card can be in fifty-two ways, the second in fifty-one ways etc. So, this formula will show how many possible positions that deck can be in:

$52 \times 51 \times 50 \times \ldots 3 \times 2 \times 1 =$

Remember, a "repeat" happens when the order of the fifty-two cards in a shuffled deck is identical to the order of the cards after any previous shuffle. So, in the second shuffle, we are hoping it matches the first; in the third shuffle, it matches the first or second, right?

The probability of a repeat in the second shuffles = $1 / 52!$ ways

The probability of a repeat in the third shuffle = $2 / 52! \times$ the probability that it did not match so far...i.e. $2/52! * (1 - 1/52!)$ and so on. After N shuffles, the probability of repeat is

$1 / 52! + 2/52! \times (1 - 1/52!) +$

$3/52! ( 1 - 2/52! \times [1 - 1/52!]) +$

When this total reaches 0.75, that is N.

What does it all mean? Cards are much more than a device for passing. Cards are the perfect mathematical stratagem that is well known to all. The fifty-two cards in a deck, divided by four suits with thirteen cards per suit are well suited, pardon the pun, for bedazzling and bewitching even the most scientifically inclined.

It is not how many tricks you know or how mechanically sound you are with a deck of cards; it is how well you can perform even the simplest of tricks. Perform one trick well, and it will fool all who watch.

---

2008), 4.

# CHAPTER TWO

## Basics of Card Magic—
## Forcing a Card

Forcing, or secretly coercing someone to choose, a specific card is the basic fundamental of card magic. The phrase "pick a card" is famous in the world and by magicians worldwide. There are many ways to get someone to choose the card you want chosen. In this book you will find many "pick a card" ideas.

## The Deck of Cards You Choose

It is crucial that you use the right deck of playing cards when you are ready to begin performing tricks. A "dollar store" deck or a paper deck will never do for professional looking tricks.

There are three different basic materials that playing cards are made of: plastic, vinyl, and paper. Plastic-coated cards are the most durable and the highest-quality cards and are used in almost all casinos. Vinyl-coated cards are a good, slightly cheaper choice, though they will bend and will not last as long as the plastic cards. Paper is the cheapest and least durable—the corners will fold, and you will have issues performing too many tricks with them.

It is important that you use high-quality cards, and plastic-coated cards are best because they are smooth and durable. Card magicians need individual cards to flow smoothly across each other and sometimes apply a zinc-based powder to lengthen the life of the cards and to make the friction between each more consistent throughout the life of the cards.

Though card magicians tend to have personal preferences of types and brands of cards based on their own experiences, the overall favorites usually have an "air cushion" or small dimples on the finish of the card in a similar manner to the dimples on a golf ball. These hold air and allow the cards to glide over one another easily.

However, over time they can collect oil and dirt, which make the cards harder to use in manipulation. Applying the powder to a card beforehand helps slow this as well as repel moisture that may build up on the hands through extended performances. Nevertheless, with time, cards will become bent and when this occurs, it is time to buy a new deck.

If possible, I would recommend using a new deck for each performance.

Here is a good tip for performing card magic: the best decks include KEM (perhaps the best in the business). Bicycle, Bee Brand, and Tally Ho are reliable decks for performing.

Once you have a reliable deck of cards, it's time to practice "forcing" someone to choose a specific card. Many beginner magicians do not try this because they think it takes too much practice, but it is the secret to many tricks. Every time you are having someone pick a card, you should try to force a card to him or her.

If you miss and they pick another card, have a different trick ready so that it does not look like you messed up. If they take the card, great! You are ready to perform a miracle.

Read their mind, locate the card, pull a prediction out of your shoe with that card on it, etc.

Let's start with the classic card force.

# Classic Force

**THE MAGIC**: Fan the cards and the spectator takes the one card for which you already know the identity. How to learn the identity is explained in detail in this book. The simplest way is to take a look at the top card then cut the deck, bringing this card to the center of the deck. The possibilities are endless for what you can do with this.

**THE MECHANICS**: Start with the card you want to force on top of the deck. Cut the deck in your hands so that the top card (force card) is now near the middle of the deck and fan the cards.

As you do this, keep an eye on where this top card is. Naturally, it is spaced out a little more than the rest of the cards. Fan the cards with one or two hands. The photos show a one-hand fan and the other shows how the cards look from underneath in a two-hand fan. Whichever is easiest or best for you is the fan you want to use.

It is okay if there is a natural gap that will help you keep your eye on the force card. If you want, you can even put a light pencil mark on the card as you are starting to learn this trick.

Start to move the cards from the left into your right hand by pulling them over with your right thumb.

Timing is the key to this. Ask the person to pick a card. As they reach up to pick a card, time it so that at about this time you get to the card you want them to take and make it easy for them to take this card.

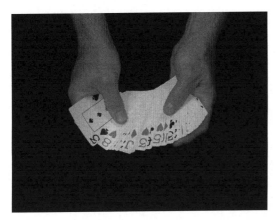 

Nonchalantly spread the cards a little more and guide this card right into their outstretched fingertips.

Practice this and you can do it anywhere, with any deck of cards, under all kinds of conditions.

# Mistaken Card Force

**THE MAGIC**: A spectator names a number from ten to thirty and the magician counts down to the card. Amazingly, it matches the previously written prediction, or you have just forced a spectator to take a card that you already know what it is, so you can proceed with your own variation.

**THE MECHANICS**: You must pretend to mess up for this to work. Place the card that you want to force to them in the seventh position in the deck. Ask them to name any number from ten to thirty. For example, they say sixteen.

Start counting cards down onto the table into a pile. One, two, three, four, keep counting but go past sixteen. Since the force card is in the seventh position, add seven to the number the spectator picked. So go to twenty-three and say, "Whoops. I went too far . . . here you had better do it! It'll be fairer that way anyway!" Pick up the twenty-three cards and put them back on the deck.

What you have just done is placed the force card in the exact position of the card they are going to stop on!

Have them do exactly what you were supposed to do and when they get to number sixteen, that will be the force card. This is a very cool idea for how to force a card.

# Dribble Force

**THE MAGIC**: Cards are being dropped from the right hand to the left. The spectator asks for the magician to stop dropping the packets of cards and the magician is then able to perform a trick culminating in him naming the chosen card.

**THE MECHANICS**: Have the card you wish to force in the upper portion of the deck and hold a break above it with the thumb in the right hand. Dribble the cards (drop a few of the cards in little packets) into the other hand asking the spectator to say stop. The speed of the dribbling should be moderate. When the spectator calls stop, drop all the cards beneath the break. Ask that he take the top card from the pile in your left hand. The force is complete.

Pace your dribble, and the spectator will certainly say stop before you run out of cards.

# 20-Count Force

**THE MAGIC**: You know the identity of a card that seems to be chosen at random.

**THE MECHANICS**: This is an automatic force, which is very handy. You need to prepare by knowing the tenth card, and then ask for a number between ten and twenty.

You deal that many cards out, creating a new stack of cards on the table.

Ask them to add the two digits together, then count that many cards out of the new stack.

The last card counted will be the card you memorized in the first place.

Ask them to remember the top card of the little stack and do whatever you what to do with this self-working force.

As an example, you have looked at the tenth card and memorized the nine of clubs. Square or straighten the deck and ask for a number between ten and twenty. They say fifteen. You count fifteen cards off the top of the deck creating a stack of fifteen cards. Pick up this stack of fifteen cards and place it back on top of the rest of the deck. They add up the five and the one of fifteen and they get six. You now count off six cards from the top of the deck. The sixth card is the nine of clubs. Try it; you will see how it works every time. Remember, it is a number between ten and twenty but cannot be the number ten or twenty.

# The Hindu Shuffle (Reverse and Forward)

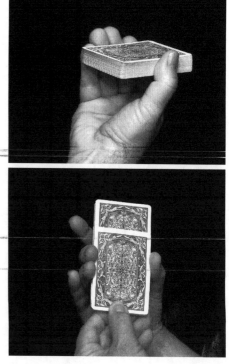

**THE MAGIC**: Although not really a trick in itself, it is often used with other tricks. In the most basic form, a card on the bottom of the deck remains on the bottom or is brought to the top while the magician appears to be mixing or shuffling the deck.

**THE MECHANICS**: For the reverse Hindu Shuffle, hold the deck facedown by the end with the thumb and middle finger on either side of the long side of the deck. For sake of demonstration, let us use the right hand.

16

The index finger can rest lightly on top for more support. The left hand comes to the top of the deck. The thumb, middle, and ring finger touch the side of the deck. The index finger stays out in front.

The left hand lightly takes packets of cards from the top of the deck. The removed cards fall onto the palm of the left hand.

The index finger stops the cards from flying forward keeping them squared somewhat in the palm of the left hand. The left hand goes to the top of the deck once more and removes another packet that falls upon the current packet in the palm of the left hand.

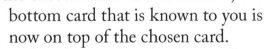

This action is repeated several times until there are only a few cards left. These are placed on top of the deck, which is then squared. This is the key. If you wanted to end up with the last two cards on the top of the deck, you would continue the packet removal until two cards were left. Then you would drop these two cards on the top of the packet in the palm of your hand. If used as a key card locator, where you want the current bottom card to be placed directly on top of a chosen card, you would begin the shuffle, and ask the chosen card to be returned at any time. Once it is returned, complete the shuffle by placing the remainder of the deck on top of the chosen card. In this manner, the bottom card that is known to you is now on top of the chosen card.

The key to this shuffle is to form a trap with the fingers so that the cards fall neatly into the palm.

The index finger is especially important, as it will stop the cards from flying everywhere. The index finger of the other hand can go where you like. I usually keep it well out of the way. It is up to you about how many packets you glide off the top. I usually drag about ten packets, then repeat the shuffle again.

With the forward Hindu Shuffle, you peek a look at the bottom card of the deck.

Starting with the deck in your hand, you remove a small stack of cards from the bottom on the deck. Let's use the left hand this time.

Reach under the deck of cards and remove a large amount of the cards from the bottom of the deck.

Bring this stack over the top of the deck and slide off the top cards of this bottom stack and drop them on top of the original deck in your left hand.

Then pull the remaining bottom cards including the one you peeked at when the shuffle began and repeat this step until the only card remaining in your right hand is the bottom card. Drop this last card, the original bottom card on the top of the deck, and you have successfully moved the bottom card, the card you peeked at on the top of the deck.

It looks as if the deck has been well shuffled when in reality you have moved the bottom card you peeked at to the top of the deck. Now that you know the card on the top of the deck you are prepared to perform any number of tricks where it is necessary to know the card you wish to force upon a spectator.

# CHAPTER THREE
## Controlling the Cards

Much like forcing a card onto an unsuspecting candidate, being able to control a card or a series of cards in the deck is another basic principle of card magic. Here are the basic moves known to the modern magician.

# Making the Pass

**THE MAGIC**: The "pass" with cards is a method of secretly cutting the deck so that a selected card may be brought at once from the middle to the top or bottom of the deck. There are many different passes with cards, some with one hand and others with both hands. The most common one is done as follows:

**THE MECHANICS**: As the card is being replaced in the deck (replaced after it has been chosen by a spectator), hold your hands well away from you, at arm's length. This is important, for it gives you more space for a "swing," and more time in which to execute the pass (more on this in a moment).

Most beginners try to make the pass with the hands stationary and close to the body. It is practically impossible to do this unobserved, as you will soon see. On the other hand, with a bit of an arm swing, I deny the average observer to see the pass when done expertly—and with a little practice, you will be an expert.

Pick up a deck of cards and hold them in your left hand. Place the little finger of the left hand over the selected card and close the deck. The second and third fingers of the left hand are above the deck, the left thumb is in its natural position at the left of the deck, and the left forefinger is curled up under the deck, out of the way.

Grasp the lower half of the deck firmly with your right fingertips pressing it firmly to the left into the crook of the left thumb. Keep up this pressure the entire time. The right thumb is at your end of the deck, and the right fingers are at the audience side. The right forefinger does not do anything. Now raise the upper portion by pushing up with your little finger on your left hand, and steadying with your next two fingers. Gripped between the little left finger and the second and third, you pull up and to the right of your left thumb and tip the right side of it sharply upward so that the edges of the two portions clear each other and the two packets blend into a complete deck. When this is accompanied by a swing toward your body, it is very hard to see because the right hand partially covers it.

This pass will bring the chosen card to the top of the deck. If you wish to bring a card to the bottom of the deck, put your little finger under the selected card instead of over it as I have just explained. By counting a few cards above or below your little finger, you can bring the card two from the top, three from the bottom or however many you desire.

This pass was once considered a basic sleight and one that all professionals needed to master. Over the years, it became forgotten and by the early part of the century became a lost art. In the late 1990s, it made a comeback and once again, all the best magicians use it.

Street magician David Blaine became a great success with his use of this one simple yet important card sleight. In fact, the phrase "sleight of hand" was coined when this trick first came into use. It has stuck with magicians ever since.

# Double Flip Card Control

**THE MAGIC**: Although not really a card trick on its own, the double flip or double lift is an important trick to know if you are working with cards.

**THE MECHANICS**: Hold the deck in your left hand with the thumb on one long side, slightly facing your audience and the fingers on the other long side slightly facing to you. With the fingers of your right hand, pick up the top two cards of the deck and flip them over to reveal what is supposed to be the face of the top card when in fact it is the second card. Then reverse the move to turn the card back over.

In order for this to be able to fool anyone, you need to be able to quickly grab hold of the top two cards before you do the flip. Once it looks natural after much practice, you will be able to make people think you are turning over the top card when in fact you are turning over the top two cards and making them look like one card. Although not a trick in itself, it's critical to the success of some card tricks. For example, let's say you want to show the top card, appear to place it in the middle of the deck, and then have it magically appear back on top.

# Stacking the Deck

**THE MAGIC**: A variety of tricks can be performed with a deck of cards that has been stacked, including naming any card picked, naming a forced card, etc.

**THE MECHANICS**: The cards are set up as per the following chart. The cards must not be shuffled, but the magician can cut the cards and have several spectators do a straight, single cut. Once you understand the set up, you will know where each card is in the deck.

The cards must be stacked as shown in the table below, by first placing the ace of clubs on to a table face up, then the four of hearts on top of it followed by the seven of spades, ten of diamonds, king of clubs, three of hearts, and so on until the whole pack is set in the master system order. When complete, turn the deck facedown. The top card is the ace of clubs and the bottom card is the jack of diamonds.

| Clubs | Hearts | Spades | Diamonds |
|-------|--------|--------|----------|
| Ace | 4 | 7 | 10 |
| King | 3 | 6 | 9 |
| Queen | 2 | 5 | 8 |
| Jack | Ace | 4 | 7 |
| 10 | King | 3 | 6 |
| 9 | Queen | 2 | 5 |
| 8 | Jack | Ace | 4 |
| 7 | 10 | King | 3 |
| 6 | 9 | Queen | 2 |
| 5 | 8 | Jack | Ace |
| 4 | 7 | 10 | King |
| 3 | 6 | 9 | Queen |
| 2 | 5 | 8 | Jack |

Clubs, hearts, spades, and diamonds is the order of the suits in the deck. Just as a heart always follows a club, a club always follows a diamond.

There are three constants, which will keep you informed of the position of each card in the deck:

1. Each card has a numerical value, ace=1, jack=11, queen=12, and king=13.

2. Each card is three numbers apart, ace, 4, 7, 10, etc.

3. Every thirteenth card is a card of the same value, but a different suit.

There are many ways you can use a stacked deck. Perform the "Chosen Card Classic," "Random Card," "Name All Four," "Mind Reader," "Find the Card," or improvise your own tricks.

# Chosen Card Classic

**THE MAGIC**: The magician names the card chosen by a spectator.

**THE MECHANICS**: Fan out the cards, ask a spectator to pick a card, and separate the deck at that point. As you move the top half to the bottom of the deck, secretly glance at the bottom card and you will instantly know the spectator's card. Simply add 3 to the bottom card value and the following suit. You now know the card value so you can improvise your own tricks from here or simply name the chosen card.

# Random Card

**THE MAGIC**: The magician puts a deck of cards behind his back and pulls out the exact card chosen by a spectator.

**THE MECHANICS**: After the spectator cuts the deck, you take the cards and glance secretly at the bottom card as you put them behind your back, ask the spectators to name a random card, and you then pull it from the deck. Simply add three to the bottom card and increment the next suit; this is the value of the top card. Count through the cards until you come to their card, where you pull it out and show them.

# Name All Four

**THE MAGIC**: The deck is cut into four piles. The magician then correctly predicts the top card of each pile.

**THE MECHANICS**: Cut the deck several times using the Hindu Shuffle (moving the bottom card to the top of the deck). With the Hindu Shuffle you know the name of the top card of the deck after the shuffle.

Ask them to separate the deck into four card piles.

Announce you are going to predict the top card off of each of the four decks. You already know the top card on the first deck pile, so start from the fourth deck pile, which is the opposite end of the known top card pile and name the card you already know. When you pick up the card, you will then be able to see its true value. Then you name that card before you pick up the second card and continue to do this until you have named all four cards. Then simply show the cards you have just named to the spectator. Once you have collected all four of the top cards, you show them to the audience and you have named all four correctly.

I often repeat them a couple of times and get the audience to repeat with you. This way they are all on the same page when you show that you accurately predicted the name of all four cards.

# Mind Reader

**THE MAGIC**: As a spectator concentrates on their chosen card, the magician reads their mind and names it.

**THE MECHANICS**: Hold the deck of cards in your right hand and slowly let them drop into the palm of your left hand, asking your spectator to say "stop" wherever they want. Secretly look at the bottom card of the remaining deck in your right hand and ask the spectator to take the top card of the deck in your left hand and memorize it. Tell them they must concentrate on their card; you then name their card.

# Find the Card

**THE MAGIC**: A spectator names a random card, and the magician announces how many cards down in the deck it is.

**THE MECHANICS**: Tell the spectator that you can tell them how many cards down in the deck their chosen card is and ask them to choose any card, number, and suit. Then locate a card with the same suit as the one named by the spectator, which is nearest to the bottom. Subtract the number chosen from the card of the same suit nearest the bottom of the deck. Then multiply the answer by four and then subtract the number of cards that were below the bottom suit card. The result is how many cards down from the deck you must count to reach the spectator's chosen card. If the chosen card is a higher value than the suit card on or nearest the bottom of the deck, just add thirteen and proceed as above.

For example: if the spectator chooses the nine of diamonds and the card with the same suit nearest the bottom is a five of diamonds, you will need to add thirteen to the five of diamonds, making eighteen. Now subtract their card, the nine of diamonds from eighteen; this leaves the number nine. Multiply nine by four, which equals thirty-six, then subtract the number two (which is the number of cards below the bottom suit card). This totals thirty-four; so the nine of diamonds is thirty-four cards down from the top of the deck.

# Easy Card Locator

This is one of the easiest ways to locate a card. If a spectator has a red-backed or blue-backed Bicycle deck of cards, you will be able to do this trick using a borrowed deck as well as using your own deck. Using a deck from a spectator is a better way to fool them because it is their own deck.

**THE MAGIC**: Ask a spectator to choose a card from the deck; if it is a borrowed deck, all the better.

After looking at the chosen card, the spectator puts it facedown on the top of the deck. Cut the deck and put the bottom half of the deck on the top; this completes the cut and buries the chosen card somewhere in the middle of the deck. The deck can be cut as many times as they like. Once the spectator is happy that their card is lost in the deck, you take the deck, riffle through it, and immediately locate their card!

**THE MECHANICS**: One of the easiest ways to find a card lost in a deck of cards is to use a locator card. The locator card we are using has been specially prepared and placed on the bottom of the deck. Take a card, and with a pair of scissors, cut the card ever so slightly shorter than the rest of the deck. This locator card is now a couple of millimeters shorter than the rest of the deck. Have this locator card ready before you begin this trick in the hopes that a spectator will provide a deck for you. When they provide a deck, secretly add it to their deck. If no deck meets the criteria listed earlier, then you use your own deck with the locator card.

A short locator card in the deck is able to locate a chosen card if the chosen card is above or below the locator card. If the chosen card was

placed on the top of the deck and the locator card was on the bottom, cutting the deck will bring the locator card on top of the chosen card. Finding the locator card with a riffle will place the chosen card to the top or bottom of the deck depending upon whether you are riffling up or down on the deck. To riffle, hold the deck as in the photo and slowly let each card drop off your finger as you drop the cards one by on onto a table.

# Finger Break

**THE MAGIC**: This in itself is not a trick; rather, it is a technique used by professional magicians. You will find it mentioned in this book and in other professional magic books.

**THE MECHANICS**: Hold the deck in your left hand palm with your pinky against the edge. By lifting a number of cards off the back edge of the deck with the right thumb, you can force the cards to stay separated by slipping your pinky between these cards and the rest of the deck. When you need to lift off those cards or remember the place, you can do it without

any problems. This move is critical when doing the doublelift and other multiple card maneuvers.

Holding the deck in this manner while performing will seem more natural if you do not bring any attention to it.

# Card Throwing

**THE MAGIC**: Magician Ricky Jay made a name for himself in the 1970s by throwing cards from the middle of the street to the top of many New York City skyscrapers. The technique takes some work but the results can be amazing. Once you have the technique down, not only will you be able to throw a card a great height or distance, you will also be able to knock down objects such as paper cups, dolls, etc.

**THE MECHANICS**: The throw is all in the wrist, and a brand new deck of high-quality cards will certainly help with the throwing. Hold the card you want to throw between your index and first fingers. Grip it between your first knuckles right after your fingernail. The rest of the card should come into your hand and be touching the palm of your hand. Bring your wrist back toward you as far as possible, like to your neck. Bend your arm back towards your chest.

With a Frisbee type throw, snap the card out of your hand. The arm motion is where your distance is going to come from. The spin you put on the card with your wrist is going to act like a gyroscope and keep the card straight. Be certain to follow through on the throw much as a baseball player or football player completes a toss.

When throwing outside, throw with the wind, not against it. Throwing inside will give good distance. At all times, keep the throw straight and parallel to the ground. Do not try to throw up or down until you have the knack.

# Bottom Glide

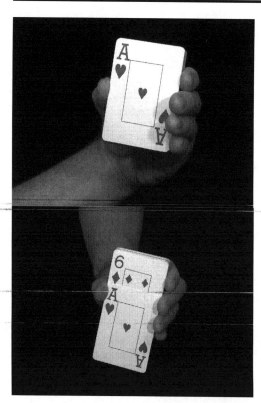

**THE MAGIC**: Bottom card is shown, then dealt onto the table where it changes to another card.

**THE MECHANICS**: As a right-handed person, you hold the deck in your left hand, palm up. The deck is face up in your palm. Your thumb is on the left side of the deck while your fingers are on the right side. Show the bottom card.

Turn your hand and the deck facedown.

During the turning motion, use your fingers to secretly pull back the bottom card about a quarter of an inch. In the photo, the pulled back card has been exaggerated to show what is happening.

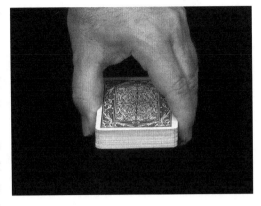

When your hand is facedown, the bottom card will be protruding towards your wrist and unseen by the audience.

Use your right hand to slide the card just above the bottom card out and onto the table. As you remove this card, your left-hand fingers move the bottom card back into place.

With this move, you are able to pull the bottom card clear so the next card can be dealt out. In this trick, we are dealing from the bottom of the deck while secretly keeping the original bottom card on the bottom.

# Palming Cards

**THE MAGIC**: The importance of basic moves and knowledge of card magic cannot be minimized. Anyone should be able to learn the mechanics of basic tricks; a true illusionist will also learn and master the basic tools of card magic. This is one of the most important of those tools.

**THE MECHANICS**: The deck is held in the left hand with the cards that are to be palmed lying on top. The thumb and third finger keep these cards in place and the little finger is under them. As the right hand approaches the left and is about three or four inches from it, the little finger pushes the cards up toward the right hand, the thumb and third finger relax their pressure, and the cards spring or shoot into the palm of the right hand, where they are retained by partly closing the hand. At the very moment the cards

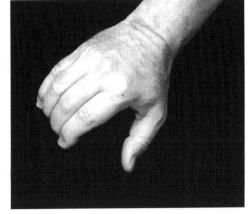

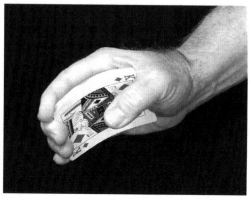

are palmed, the left hand moves away slowly. This move, which is also known as the spring palm, is imperceptible.

Should the magician wish to hand the deck to a member of the audience with his right hand, in which the cards are palmed, he places the left-hand little finger under the card or cards that are to be palmed. The right hand grasps the deck between the thumb and the second finger, as if to make the "pass." The cards that are to be palmed are pushed by the left hand little finger into the right palm. Then the wrist of the left hand is turned outward, while the right hand grasping the deck at the left hand upper corner between the thumb and first finger hands it to the one who waits for it.

# Bottom Palm

**THE MAGIC**: Much like the normal palming move, this one is a palm from the bottom of the deck.

**THE MECHANICS**: In this method of palming a card, the deck lies lengthwise in the left hand, the lower end in the fork of the thumb, the upper end against the first joints of the second and third fingers, and the tip of the left thumb resting on the face of the cards.

As the right hand approaches to take the deck, the fingers of the left hand press slightly against the bottom of the deck, and then partly close. The result is that the bottom card of the deck is separated from the rest of the deck and is retained in the left palm by the bent fingers, while the right hand removes the rest of deck.

# CHAPTER FOUR

## Revealing the Chosen Card

In card magic, there are two basic principles: you find and reveal a chosen card or you perform some sort of trick that does not include an audience member choosing a card. Here are the tricks today's professionals use when they want to find the chosen card.

# Three Chosen Cards

**THE MAGIC**: To me, the best magic tricks are those that leave both the magician and the audience amazed. This trick is just that: amazing. It sounds too good to be true and yet, it works every time.

With a standard deck of cards, have three participants each select one card without showing it to you. Instruct them to remember their card. All three cards are placed randomly back into the deck and the deck is mixed. All the cards are dealt out in a disorderly fashion, and in the end, the last three cards will be the chosen cards.

**THE MECHANICS**: Three cards are chosen by three different people. Divide up the rest of the deck into three stacks of cards. Stack one has ten cards facedown. Next to it, deal a stack of fifteen cards, then next to that deal another fifteen-card stack. Keep the remaining nine cards in your hand.

Ask the first participant to put their card on top of the ten-card stack. Allow them to take as many cards as they wish from the second stack, placing those on top of their card.

Ask the second participant to put their card on the middle stack. This person may take any amount of cards from the third stack and place them on top of their card.

Ask the third participant to put their card on top of the third stack. Give them the nine cards you have been holding on to, and have them put these cards on top of their card.

Pick up the third stack, place it on the middle stack, and put both on top of the first stack. Explain what is obvious, that the three chosen cards are now lost within the deck.

Proceed to take four cards off the top and place them on the bottom of the deck. There is no need to discuss this event; it is simply the start of your trick.

You are now going to separate the entire deck into two stacks: one face up and one facedown. Beginning with the top card, turn this card face up and beside it turn the next card facedown. Always begin the process with the top card going to the face up stack. Continue the process and repeat it until all the cards in your hand are gone. The entire deck has now been divided between two stacks on the table; one face up and one facedown. Let your audience know that they should tell you if they happen to see their card in the face up stack. (This, by the way, cannot happen because of the system you have used.)

Pick up the face up stack and move it to one side. It is no longer needed for the trick. Pick up the facedown deck and once again split it into two stacks, one face up and one facedown.

Once again, place the face up stack away and begin the process with the facedown stack and repeat this until you have only three cards left, facedown.

Turn these three cards over, and reveal their selected cards. The top one is the third participant's card, the subsequent is the second participant's card, and the bottom one is the first participant's card. This system is foolproof and if you try this on your own without participants, you might even fool yourself.

Alternatively, you can start the trick by showing three aces; I would suggest the two red aces and the ace of spades. I like the ace of spades because unlike the other aces, the spade is normally huge. Perform the trick as usual, but instead of having three people each choose a card, use the three aces as the chosen cards. This is a good alternative if you perform this trick on TV or stage, or if you perform the trick for less than three people.

# Card or Watch in a Bottle

**THE MAGIC**: The magician shows an empty, plastic one-liter soda bottle, the cap securely closed on top. He borrows a card or watch and makes it magically appear inside the sealed bottle. The only way to remove the card or watch is to cut the bottle open.

Note: This trick can be performed with anything, from a coin to an iPod. It can even use a combination of several items.

The secret set up and moves: Slide the bottle label down the bottle and with a knife or scissors (ask for permission and help from an adult) cut a slit into the bottle. Work on the slit until it is one half-inch wide and the height of the label. Slide the label back into place, so it covers the hole, and make a one-inch slit in the label over the center of the opening in the bottle.

In order to get the watch into the bottle, you will need to push the watch through the label slit and on through the larger slit in the bottle. The move to push the watch into the bottle needs to be done quickly. Practice in front of a mirror until you can do it well.

**THE MECHANICS**: In order to hide the fact that the bottle and label have been altered, hold the bottle with your hand over the slit. Say, "This is a plastic bottle; the cap has been screwed down tight." As you talk, show the bottle all around. Ask to borrow a watch and say, "It is impossible for a solid to penetrate a solid, but I will show you how it is done."

Use the watch to tap all over the bottle, showing that the bottle is solid and that the watch cannot possibly penetrate it. Switch the bottle and the watch so that they are now in opposite hands. When you change hands, keep the slit hidden, but position the bottle so that you will be able to thrust the watch through the slit.

Keep holding the bottle with the slit facing you. Tap a few more times, and on the last tap, using a quick thrust, push the watch through the slit and into the bottle. The sound of your hand hitting the bottle and the watch clanking around inside the bottle should mask the sound of the watch going through the slit.

Move the bottle back to its original hand and position while shaking the bottle to show that the watch is now inside. Turn the bottle upside down, remove the cap and try to shake out the watch. Obviously, it will not come out.

Pick up a pair of scissors or knife (perhaps with the help of a parent) and cut the bottle open, making the first cut at the location of the original slit. Be certain to cut up the area of the original slit in order to disguise the fact that there was a slit there before the trick began. After cutting the bottle, the watch will fall out and the audience can now inspect the watch and bottle remnants.

# Clock, Time, and Pick a Card

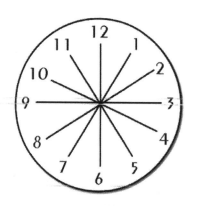

**THE MAGIC**: Here is a great trick that you can make at home. The magician shows the cut out face of a clock. Next to each number on the clock is a facedown card. Ask someone to secretly choose any number on the clock. Then they choose the number across from it, subtract the smaller number from the larger one and you reveal the answer every time and then reveal the card at the chosen point.

**THE MECHANICS**: Begin by making clocks such as the three clock faces below. The trick is completely self-working; all you need are the three clock faces and your own presentation.

The magician shows the first clock face and says, "Select any number on the clock. You have a complete free choice. Remember your number and don't tell me what it is. Got it?"

Show the second clock face and say, "Follow the straight line from your number, through the center of the clock and to the number on the other side. Take the two numbers that are connected by the line and subtract the smaller number from the larger one. You now have a new number. Please remember it. And don't tell me what the new number is."

"Ready. I have your new number on the last clock face." Show the last clock face which only has the number six on it and you have managed to fool them with this clever magic trick.

For added effect, reveal the name of the card that is facedown at the six. (As you set up this trick, you should have peeked at that card and memorized it.)

# Pop-Up Card, the Complete Effect

**THE MAGIC**: A card is freely chosen from a shuffled deck and returned to the deck. Once returned, half of the chosen card is left protruding out of the end at about the center of the deck. The deck is then placed halfway down in the card case and held there by pressure from the magician's thumb and fingertips. The selected card is pushed down level with the rest of the deck. Upon releasing the thumb and finger pressure on the deck, all the cards drop into the case with the exception of the selected card, which seems to pop up out of the deck.

**THE MECHANICS**: In order to achieve this trick, you will need a little preparation. Remove the small side flaps of the card case. Choose any card in the deck, perhaps a joker, and cut a slit down the middle of the card from the end to the center, a distance of about 1-1¾ inches. On the upper left hand corner of the card, make a pencil dot in order to locate this card later.

Set up the deck by removing six cards from it. Then place the slit card, slit side up, into the deck, second from the bottom. You remove the cards in order to lighten the load and to make the cards fit more loosely into the box.

To perform the trick, bring the deck case out of your pocket and remove the cards. Fan the cards so all can see. The slit should be covered with other cards in the natural fan formation. Ask for a card to be freely chosen from the fan. Cut the deck after the card has been removed, this will bring the card with the slit to the center area of the deck. Fan the cards again and locate the slit card by sighting the pencil dot on the upper left hand corner. Take back the chosen card with its back facing you and insert it in the slit of the prepared card. This move is not difficult since the card above and below it covers the slit card. It is made easier when you bear down on the upper left hand corner of the slit card with the selected card, forcing the left upper half of the card down and opening the slit for the card to be inserted. The slit keeps the selected card from going down into the deck more than halfway. Square the deck with the card protruding. Turn the cards around so the faces of the cards are toward the audience and place the deck into the card case that is first shown to be empty. The deck only goes in halfway and is held in place in the card case by the right thumb and fingers. With the left forefinger, push the selected card into the deck and level with the rest of the deck. This will force the slit card down into the bottom of the case. Hold the deck supported with the pressure of the right thumb on one side of the case and the fingers on the other.

Hold the deck and case upright, release your grip, the entire deck will slide down into the box with the gravitational pull but the chosen card will appear to pop up out of the deck. You can remove it from the deck and give it out for inspection. Close the box and put it back in your pocket.

# Ace Shake-Up

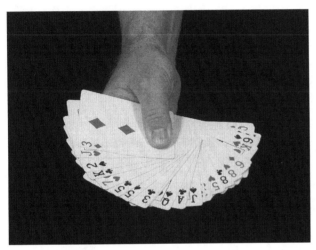

**THE MAGIC**: This trick was performed on television where the magician had the spectator sign a card, the card was put back in the pack and the chosen card was made to appear from between two aces.

**THE MECHANICS**: Hand the two red aces to a member of the audience and ask them to hold them. Fan out the deck, face out, and ask someone else to choose a card by touching it. Square the deck up, leaving the chosen card stuck out to be signed and then shown to the rest of the audience.

After the spectator has signed the chosen card, secretly put it into "palm position," when you square up the deck so you can easily palm the card when you want to. The palm position requires that the chosen card is sticking out of the lower corner of the pack meeting your inner thumb. Palm the chosen card as you hand them the deck.

Have them mix the deck all they like. After they are convinced that the card is well lost in the deck, ask for the two aces and sandwich the palmed card between them, showing only the aces face up.

Ask them to hold the deck openly, fan out the cards and start to shake the aces directly over the pack, ask them to watch as their card rises from the deck into the two aces, shake a little more loosely and the card will appear to their amazement, shaking out from between the two aces.

# The Card between the Jokers— Johnny Carson's Trick

**THE MAGIC**: The cards are spread out between the magician's hands and the spectator is instructed to touch one card somewhere in the middle of the pack. The touched card is turned face up. The deck is squared up, and the spectator cuts the deck several times. The jokers find the card! One joker is on top of the card, and one joker is right below the selected card. Truly a card masterpiece!

**THE MECHANICS**: First, get the jokers on the top and bottom of the deck as you shuffle the cards (you can pretend to count the cards to "make sure they are all there" or something.) Do not make it obvious. Once the jokers are on the top and bottom of the pack, do a couple fake shuffles and keep the jokers where they are. You can do a quick overhand shuffle and just leave the two cards in their place.

Every good card trick becomes much better with a good shuffle.

Spread the cards out between your hands (as if you would if you were fanning the cards in your hand).

Ask the spectator to touch one card.

Jog the chosen card out about an inch. (This means move the card toward them, but without removing it from the deck.) Now if they touched a card near the middle, you should have about half the cards held in the left hand, and half in the right, but still in the fanned out position.

the right, but still in the fanned out position.

Use the cards in your right hand to push down on the right side of the selected card and the left hand's cards to push up on the left side of it. This should flip the chosen card face up while the other cards are still facedown. Have them remove their card, look at it and then place it on top of the deck face up. You have squared the deck while they were looking at their card.

Once their card is on the top of the squared up deck, have the spectator cut the deck as many times as they want (single cuts only).

Now spread the cards out again, facedown on the table. Pause. Say something like, "Ohhhhhh the seven of diamonds!" That is the only face up card and it's their card. At this point, it does not look like anything magic has happened. But you know that their card sandwiched between the jokers, and the hard work is done. This is true since the jokers were on the top and the bottom of the deck. By placing the chosen card on the top of the top joker, no number of deck cuts will undo the sandwich of joker, chosen card, and joker.

Okay, fun time. Place the squared deck on the table. Wave your hands over the deck and do something that looks a little magical. Have a member of the audience speak to the deck and say, "Jokers, find the card!"

Build up the drama with the actions you feel most comfortable with when it comes to creating excitement in your act. Spread the deck facedown across the table and pull the chosen card and the two cards sandwiching above and below it away from the deck but don't show that it is jokers on both sides of the chosen card.

Turn all the other cards face up to show that there are no jokers remaining in the deck of cards, or better yet, make two stacks of cards. "No jokers here. No jokers in this pile either!" Have them turn over the cards right above and the card right below the chosen card. Yes, the jokers have found the card!

Most decks have two jokers, some have three and some have four. The idea is the same, always sandwich the chosen card between whatever number of jokers that are in the deck. If you don't have jokers, use aces or kings. Anything that will sandwich the chosen card.

Here is an extra tip on making this magic trick even more successful... give all the credit to the jokers. Have a round of applause for the jokers. Thank the jokers personally. This makes it a more memorable magic trick, your audience will give you more credit for not being a self-centered magician, and they will like you even more.

# The Cards and the Floating Match

**THE MAGIC**: Show an ordinary pack of playing cards. Spread the deck and remove one card. Take this card and place an unprepared match on top of it. Wave your hand over the match and the match will begin to float upward off the card.

It continues to float two inches above the card. While the match is floating, take another card and swipe it above, then under the match to show it really is unsupported and has no strings attached.

The match slowly floats back down again at the magician's command.

**THE MECHANICS**: For this card trick effect you will need an ordinary pack of playing cards and some invisible string. Any good magic store will stock some.

Take any card from the deck and a length of invisible thread. With clear tape, stick one end of the thread to the face of the card in the bottom left hand corner. Tightly wind the thread around the card about three times, then stick the other end to the opposite corner on the face of the card.

You should end up with a playing card with about three lengths of invisible thread running across the back of the card.

To finish the gimmick, stick another card over the face of the original card with glue or double stick tape to hide the strings on the face.

Playing cards where the pattern covers the whole back (without a white border) are the best for this trick. A complete, busy background hides the invisible thread perfectly.

To have the effect, you need to make it look as if are randomly picking a card from the deck. To do this, have the gimmicked card in the middle of the deck before you begin the trick.

Since this card is double the thickness of a normal card, it is very easy to locate in the deck. Riffle through the deck and stop at the gimmicked card, or spread the deck on a table, then take out the gimmicked card.

Hold the card facedown in your hand between your thumb and fingers. Place the match on top of the card across all three invisible thread strings.

To make the match float upward slowly push the edges of the card together so it begins to bend downward. The card will come away from the match but the invisible string will hold the match up, giving the illusion the match is floating.

At this point you can take another card and swipe it over the top of the match then push it under the match (and under the strings) to prove nothing is supporting it.

To make the match float back down, simply move your thumb and fingers slowly apart again. The playing card will straighten out and the match will look like it is floating back down.

As soon as you have finished the trick, place the gimmicked card back into the deck and give it a shuffle. This technique has hidden the gimmicked card back into the deck.

# Standard Card Trick

**THE MAGIC**: Shuffle a deck of cards and invite a spectator to take one. Once they have memorized the card, they place it back on top of the deck and you give the whole deck another shuffle.

Randomly go through the deck and choose a card. Show it to your audience and then look dejected when it turns out not to be the chosen card. It appears that the magician has failed to perform the trick.

Take the incorrect card and give it a snap, then it will change into the chosen card.

**THE MECHANICS**: The snap of the "wrong" card is the secret to the success of this trick. The speed at which the snap is achieved is so fast your eye cannot follow the cards turning round, so it looks like they instantly change.

Use one of the techniques from chapter 2 to control the cards. Shuffle the cards and ask a spectator to choose one. Once they have memorized the card, ask them to place the card on top of the deck.

Next, shuffle a card on top of the spectator's chosen card. Jog this top card towards you about half an inch. The card now overhangs the back of the deck slightly. This card acts as a marker, marking the chosen card.

In an apparent squaring up action, grab a break beneath the jogged card, take it and the chosen card and place them on top of the deck. The chosen card is back on the top of the deck, just below the marker card.

# The Card Robbers—Harry Houdini's Only Invention

**THE MAGIC**: The four jacks (or kings or nines) act as robbers who successfully rob a bank (the deck) and make a miraculous getaway! Each jack goes into a different place in the deck, and as the police come, they all rise to the top and get away! This is a great beginner magic trick and a favorite of Houdinis throughout his entire life.

**THE MECHANICS**: First, prepare for the trick by removing the four jacks, as well as three random cards. Position the four jacks fanned out in your right hand with the three indifferent cards behind the last jack.

To your audience, this should look like only four jacks. Hide those other cards behind one of the jacks and lay the rest of the deck facedown in front of you.

As you show the jacks, say, "Let me tell you a little story about how the jacks robbed a bank. They climbed to the roof of the bank late at night when the bank was closed." Place all seven cards on the top of the facedown deck. It should look like you just placed four jacks on top of the deck.

Say, "The first jack went to the basement and stole all the jewels." Take the top indifferent card and slide it into the deck near the bottom. Do not let the audience actually see this card. Remember that they just saw them, and do not make this sneaky.

Say, "The second jack went to the first floor and stole all the money." Take the next card (the one on top of the deck now) and place it into the middle of the deck.

Say, "The third jack went to the top floor and stole all the gold." Place the third indifferent card near the top of the deck.

Say, "The last jack stayed on the roof and kept an eye out for the police." Pick up the last jack and casually flash the face of the jack to the audience. Make it look like this was not deliberate, and only show it so that they barely see it. What we want to do here is give the impression that you showed them all the other jacks as they recreate this trick in their minds later.

Say, "Then the cops came! Lucky for the jacks, the last jack had a whistle and blew it as he jumped up and down on the roof." Illustrate this with the top jack by picking it up and having it merrily dance around as it faces the audience.

Say, "All the jacks rushed to the top and escaped into the night." As you do this, one by one flip over the jacks on the top of the deck and toss them onto the table face up. It adds to the effect if you can make them spin a little as they land.

# The Heat Is On

**THE MAGIC**: The cards are spread out between the magician's hands and the spectator is instructed to take a card from anywhere in the pack. The card is replaced and the deck is squared. By "feeling the heat" on the backs of each of the cards, the magician is able to tell which was the last card selected.

Read on for a few cool variations. You can practically do the same trick three times with three different endings and it will seem like three completely different tricks!

**THE MECHANICS**: First, let your audience member shuffle the deck. Shuffling always adds to an already good card trick. When a spectator freely shuffles the deck, it makes everything seem that much more magical when the magician does a trick. Fan the cards out in the best way that you know how, and ask your friend to select any card from anywhere in the entire deck. As they take it out, square up the deck. Cut the deck somewhere in the middle, taking the top half with your right hand. Tell them to look at their card and remember it.

Outstretch your left hand, and have them set the card down on that half of the deck. While they are doing this (or while they were looking at their card, whichever is less obvious), glimpse the card on the bottom of the pack in your right hand and remember it. After the chosen card has been placed facedown on the packet in your left hand, drop the right hand-packet on top of the left-hand packet. Once again, hand the deck to your friend and tell them to cut the deck. Complete the cut by placing the top half on the bottom. They can do this as many times, as they want, but only single cuts at a time. This will not affect the order of the cards. Take the deck back.

What you have just done is placed a key card right above their card. You do not know the identity of their card, but since you know the card right above it, it is just as good! Now, there are several finishes to this trick. All of your work is practically done, and here is where your acting ability is put to use. Make these finishes as dramatic as possible, act as if you are amazed, and what an incredible sleight-of-hand artist you are.

Feel the Heat:

Pretend to feel the heat that they left on the card when they touched it. Set the deck down and slowly feel the back of each card, turning them over and tossing them, face up, into a pile off to the side. They will be watching your eyes; so do NOT look at the pile. Instead, stare at the facedown deck, and use your side vision to just glimpse the card. Pretend to be concentrating on the facedown deck. The longer it takes, the more dramatic it can be. When you see the "key card" tossed off to the side, pause. Take a deep breath. Say, "This is it!" and let them turn over the next card. They will be amazed.

Feel the Pulse:

This is a great variation. Although it is pretty much the same trick, the audience will think it is a different trick entirely. Just do not do these two tricks directly in a row.

Spread the cards face up across the table. Ask your friend to point with his index finger. Grab their wrist as if you are going to feel their pulse increase as their finger slides across their card. Make several passes back and forth across the spread. Slow down the motion and stop on the card that is directly above the "key card." Touch their finger to their card. They will think you can really feel their pulse increase. They will be amazed.

# Card from the Pocket

**THE MAGIC**: The magician puts the whole deck into his pocket and eventually pulls out the one "freely" chosen card by the volunteer.

**THE MECHANICS**: This is a psychological card force, similar to the forces taught in chapter 2. First, look at either the top or the bottom card in the deck and remember it.

You will force them to either pick the top or bottom card. Here is how it works.

Tell the spectator, "Choose a color . . . red or black."

Let us assume the card you want them to choose is the five of hearts. If they say red, say "Great!" and move on. If they say black, say "Great! That leaves . . . Red. Right?"

"Yes."

"Okay, red it is."

"Now let us decide if we want it high or low. When I snap my fingers, you say 'High 7, 8, 9, 10, Jack, Queen, King,' or 'Low ace, 2, 3, 4, 5, 6.'"

If they say high, say, "Great! High is eliminated!" If they say low, say "Great! Low it is!"

Are you getting the hang of this?

Have them name a few different cards in the last step. Proceed as you did above, narrowing it down to the five of hearts.

Remember, stay excited about their choices, and do not ever hesitate. Although this trick has a simple secret, it is very difficult to do flawlessly and without pause or hesitation.

In the end, pull the one card out of your pocket as you pretend to feel around the shuffled deck for it. Voila! The five of hearts!

# Slap That Fist

**THE MAGIC**: A card is chosen and lost in the deck. Five cards are taken out of the deck and placed into the spectator's fist between the first and second fingers. The cards are slapped out of the fist, and one card remains. It is the chosen card.

**THE MECHANICS**: Use "The Heat Is On" (see page 46) or the "Classic Force" (see page 13) to lose a card in the deck.

Look through the deck and grab four indifferent cards as well as the chosen card.

Place the chosen card on the bottom of the stack of these five cards. Place the cards between the first and second knuckles of the spectator's outstretched fist. To make sure you know exactly where to place the cards, I will try to explain a little further.

If someone was going to punch you with their fist, and this was all going on in slow motion, you could fit cards into their fist. Just imagine yourself sliding the cards in between the cracks in their knuckles. This is where the cards go.

Count to three: "One, Two, Three!"

Slap the cards as if you were giving someone five. Smack! The bottom card is the one that will stay in the fist. You have to hit it hard, but still be gentle.

Obviously, this is one trick you will have to practice on yourself to get both the right fist tension and the slapping motion down.

Turn over the last remaining card. "Is this your card?" Or come up with a better saying for this trick like, "Yippee, here is your card!"

This is a truly amazing effect.

# World's Greatest Card Trick

**THE MAGIC**: The magician spreads a deck of cards on the table facedown. A card is chosen and slid out of the deck. The magician squares up the deck. The spectator looks at the chosen card, shows it around and then, as the magician is randomly shuffling the deck, the card is returned. Again, the deck is squared up and spread across the table facedown. This time, a single card has a blue back while all the other cards have a red back. The deck is cut at the blue-backed card, bringing it to the top of the cards, which are squared up. This card is turned over to reveal the card previously chosen by the spectator. "Want to see it again?" asks the magician. He takes the blue-backed card and lies it facedown on the table. The magician begins to shuffle the deck again. At some point, the spectator is shown another card, asked to memorize it, and the magician continues to shuffle. The deck is squared up again and spread out. This time, no blue-backed card is in the deck. "Was this your card?" the magician asks. He then proceeds to turn over the blue-backed card removed previously from the deck and it has changed to the second chosen card.

**THE MECHANICS**: Two basic moves are used; one is the Hindu Shuffle (see page 16) and the other is the double flip (see page 21). The deck is also prepared with two of the same card with different colored backs. Any card can be used; I will use the four of diamonds in order to further demonstrate this trick. Place the blue-backed four of diamonds on the very bottom of the deck with the regular red-backed four of diamonds just above it.

Spread the deck out on the table being careful not to show the blue-backed four of diamonds on the bottom of the deck. Have a spectator choose a card, and then quickly square up the deck. The two fours of diamonds are on the bottom of the deck. The spectator looks at his chosen card, shows it around and memorizes it. Let us pretend it is the ten of clubs.

Begin the Hindu shuffle and ask the spectator to return the card to the deck as you are doing the shuffle. Place the two fours of diamonds on top of the chosen card. Square the deck and spread it on the table. Cut the deck at the blue-backed card and square the deck. The blue-backed four of diamonds is on the top while the red-backed four of diamonds is on the bottom. Perform the double flip, revealing the ten of clubs, then place it (them) back on the deck and move the blue-backed top card to the table.

Do the trick again by performing a few rounds of the Hindu shuffle, stopping to show the bottom card which is the red-backed four of diamonds, complete the shuffling without doing the Hindu shuffle, square the deck and spread it on the table. Of course, the red-backed four of diamonds does not stand out from any other card. Point to the blue-backed card previously removed from the deck. The card is thought to be the ten of clubs, turn it over to reveal that is it the four of diamonds.

# David Blaine's Card through the Window

**THE MAGIC**: The magician asks the spectator to pick a card and be careful not to allow the magician to see the face of the card, after which the spectator puts the card back into the deck.

The deck is shuffled and the magician is unsuccessful in locating the chosen card.

After a few attempts, the magician throws the cards against a plate glass window behind the spectator. Magically, the chosen card sticks to the window.

**THE MECHANICS**: You need two identical packs of cards and an accomplice.

When Blaine performed this trick on television, the effect took place in a coffee shop. You can perform this trick in any sort of environment where the location has large glass-paned windows such as a coffee shop, department store, etc. The magician and the spectator will be on the inside of the establishment and you will need to have a walking area on the outside of the window such as a sidewalk. Think of a street side coffee shop and you will get the picture.

Start with a spectator who is seated at a table with their back to the window. Ask them to choose a card from a deck, memorize it, and without showing you, replace the card in the deck.

The deck is freely shuffled and a couple of "is this your card" attempts are made, followed by a look of disbelief when the spectator tells you that it is not their card. This is all part of the act, as you do not even need to know the card.

After a few attempts, you square up the deck, feign disbelief, and throw the deck broadside at the window. The cards will hit the window and fall to the ground, all except the chosen card, which has remained stuck to the other side, the outside of the window.

The success of this trick is fully dependent upon your accomplice. They were watching from the outside and when they saw the chosen card, the accomplice finds the duplicate in their own pack and sticks the card to the window facing into the coffee shop. Then they walked away.

A small piece of looped sticky tape, wax, or white glue has attached to the duplicate card to the outer side of the window. The accomplice should then have walked away from the window.

# Stunning Card Trick

**THE MAGIC**: Two spectators each select and sign a card. One signature is signed on the face of a card and the other signature is placed on the back of the other card. Both cards are then placed facedown on the table.

Hand the card signed on the back to a spectator and have him hold it in the palm on one hand while he covers it with the palm of his other hand, sandwiching the card. Hand the other card to the other spectator and have him wave his card over the other card in the air. After a moment, he will look at his card and will see that his signature has vanished from his card, and when the other spectator looks at his card that he is holding between his hands, the other spectator's signature has appeared on the face of this card. Both signatures have mysteriously appeared on one card.

**THE MECHANICS**: A deck of cards and a duplicate card from another deck of the same brand is needed.

Place the duplicate card on top of the deck, followed by the matching card from the deck. Let us use the six of clubs. Both sixes are on the top of the deck.

Have a spectator pick any card and then force the six of clubs on the other spectator. Replace the cards as follows from the top down: forced, selected, duplicate.

Double lift to show the freely selected card and have the first spectator sign the face. Return both cards to the deck and then place the top card, not the signed card, the duplicate six of clubs, facedown on the table.

Double lift again to show the forced six of clubs card. Turn the cards over and have the second spectator sign the back. He has signed the back of the freely chosen card.

Just like before, return both cards to the deck and then place the top card on the table. Give the card with the signature on the back into the hands of the spectator that signed it.

The first spectator picks up the other card, "his" card, facedown and waves it over the card the other spectator is holding.

When he turns his card over, his signature has vanished from the face of the card.

Then, when the other spectator looks at his card, his signature is still on the back, but when he turns it over, the other spectator's signature has appeared on the face of the card.

# Back on Top

This trick is similar to the Full View Vanish (see page 69).

**THE MAGIC**: A spectator is asked to pick a card and return it to the top of the deck. The magician shows that the card is on the top of the deck, removes it and puts it in the middle of the deck. Magically it rises back to the top.

**THE MECHANICS**: The magician will ask any spectator to select a card freely. Once they have selected the card and while they are looking at it, palm the top card off the deck. This must be practiced in front of a mirror to make the palm look like you were simply squaring the deck. Let the spectator place their card on top of the deck.

Take the card still palmed in your hand and place it on top of the deck. The most natural look is for you to square the deck, then, at that instant, just place it on top. It should look as if you simply squared the deck.

Do a double flip to show the spectator's card (see page 21). The audience will think the chosen card is still on top, but in reality, you are showing the second card, not the first.

Repeat this procedure and flip those two cards back facedown on the top of the deck. From the spectator's point of view, their card is still on the top of the deck.

Take the real first card and place it in the middle of deck; this leaves the spectator's card on top, as they think it has just traveled to the center of the deck. Do another double flip to show that the chosen card is gone. Flip them back, tap the deck, remove the top card, and, like magic, the chosen card has risen from the middle of the deck back to the top.

# The Four Kings

**THE MAGIC**: Four kings are placed on the top of the deck. Each king is slipped into the deck in a variety of locations. The deck is mixed and the four kings all join up together.

**THE MECHANICS**: Take the four kings, and place one card on top of them. Fan these and show them as the four kings only, keeping the top card hidden. Place the stack of the four kings along with the hidden card on the top of the deck.

"Once upon a time there were four kings who were so fond of each other that they held a reunion every year. One of the kings was from

China." (Put the indifferent top card in the lower third of the deck. Your audience will think that this is one of the kings.)

"Another was the king of India." (Put the next card, a king, on the bottom of the deck.)

"The one who lived in India went to South America on a trip." (Pretend to place the King already on the bottom into the deck at about the upper third of the deck. In actuality, slip it back with your forefinger, and take the next-to-the-bottom card instead. This is the bottom glide technique explained on page 29.)

"Not knowing this, a third King went to visit his fellow king in India." (Move another king from the top of the deck to the bottom.) "But when I went to visit the last remaining king right here in—" (in the town in which you are currently residing) "I found them all together."

Cut the deck several times, making sure no Kings are on the bottom of the deck when the cutting is done. It is unlikely there will be, but if so, cut again and spread the deck face up on the table. All four kings will be together.

# Quick as a Wink

**THE MAGIC**: A spectator chooses a card and is asked to put it facedown onto the table under his finger and it remains in view at all times. The magician takes the top card off the deck and shows it around. The magician taps the spectator's hand with the card from the top of the deck, and then reveals it has changed to the card selected by the spectator. The spectator looks under his finger and finds the card that was at the top of the deck is now under his finger. The two cards have changed places right before his eyes.

**THE MECHANICS**: You need two of the same card on the top of the deck such as two tens of clubs. Same card, same back.

Ask the spectator to choose a card from somewhere in the center of the deck. While the spectator is looking at the selected card, secretly palm the top card of the deck. Ask the spectator to place their card on top of

the deck. Bring the hand with the palmed card down on top of the deck as you square up the deck, secretly placing the palmed card on top of the selected card. The deck is now set up with the ten of clubs, the spectator's card, and the duplicate ten of clubs on the top of the deck.

Lift up the top two cards as one with a double flip. Explain that you will put the selected card facedown on the table and the spectator will put their finger on top of it. The card is facedown as you slide it off the deck and remains facedown during the trick.

Replace both of the cards on top of the deck, put the top card on the table, and have the spectator put their finger on top. You have placed one of the ten of clubs onto the table under their finger.

Once again, lift up the top two cards as one, and put both cards back on top of the deck. Lift up the top card and tap it on the spectator's hand. The top card was the card originally chosen by the spectator. When you tap it against his hand, hold the card facedown.

Turn it over, revealing that it has "changed" to the selected card. Ask the spectator to turn over the card under their finger, and it is the other card. The cards have changed places right before their eyes, quick as a wink.

# The Royal Queen

**THE MAGIC**: The magician cuts the deck into four stacks; the spectator freely chooses a card from the top of any stack. The magician mixes the stacks together and locates the chosen card.

**THE MECHANICS**: Prearrange the deck by placing a queen on the bottom.

Shuffle a pack of cards keeping the queen in place at the bottom of the pack. Then cut the deck into at least four stacks placed facedown on a table. Keep track of the bottom stack, the one with the queen on the bottom. Ask a spectator to select a card from any of the stacks. It can be the top card or any card from any stack. They remove the card and look at it. They replace the card on top of any of the stacks.

Reassemble the deck by putting the bottom pile on top of the selected card. Now the queen from the bottom is a key card since it is directly over the chosen card.

Should the spectator place their card on top of the pile with the queen, ask him to cut the pile in order to better conceal his card and then go about reassembling the deck. This will ensure that the queen will still be on top of their card. Once the deck has been reassembled, cut it up several times, then spread out the cards face up on the table. Search for your queen, which is now below the chosen card. You can now find or name the chosen card. You can obviously use any card; it does not need to be a queen, and I have chosen to use a queen in this case just for reference sake.

# Webster's Dictionary

**THE MAGIC**: A spectator chooses a card, returns it to the deck and then spells it. As the magician deals one card for each letter, the chosen card is revealed.

**THE MECHANICS**: Ask a spectator to choose a card, and then return it to the top of the deck after they show it around and memorize it. Shuffle up the deck but keep control of the chosen card on the top of the deck.

Explain that you will locate the card by spelling it out. Ask the spectator to spell out their card, letter by letter. As they spell it out, deal one card down onto a pile for each letter. If they chose the queen of clubs, you will deal out twelve cards, one for each letter.

On the last card, which will be the "s," announce that this should be the selected card and show it to the spectator. This will not be the chosen card, you have made a mistake, or was it a spelling mistake? Okay, maybe you both made a mistake. Gather the cards together and put them back on top of the deck. This time the magician spells out the queen of clubs and this time the last card is the chosen card.

The trick works because you have reversed the order of the cards moving the top card, the selected card to the bottom of the "spelt out" pile. When you spell it out the second time, you reverse the order and the last card was the top card from the deck, which is the chosen card.

# Card in the Frame

**THE MAGIC**: A chosen card appears in the center of a frame.

**THE MECHANICS**: Buy a small frame at the dollar store and cut two pieces of black cardboard. The cardboard needs to be shiny black on one side and white on the other side. Check with artist supply stores for the right cardboard.

One piece of cardboard goes into the frame as the background. The second piece of cardboard is cut to fit over the glass of the frame and rest within the framework. Place the card you want to use in the trick into the frame. When you cover the frame with the second piece of cardboard, it will look as if the frame is empty. You also need a large white handkerchief or kitchen towel.

Start by forcing a card on a spectator, this will be the same card that you have hidden in the frame. Once the card is returned to the deck, place the deck back into its box and put it into your pocket or away in a drawer.

Pick up the frame covered with the handkerchief, show that the frame is empty being careful not to disturb the false black piece covering the glass of the frame. Cover the frame again and lie it facedown on the handkerchief.

Ask for the name of the card or simply name the card yourself. As the finale, tap the back of the frame and lift it up to reveal that the chosen card is now in the frame, behind the glass. When you lift the frame, simultaneously slide the handkerchief off the table taking the false cardboard with you.

You can hand out the frame to show that the card is certainly sealed in there.

Another option in this trick is to use a mirror rather than black cardboard in the frame. A second piece of mirror will cover the frame and the card within. Although the mirror looks better than the black cardboard, there is a danger of dropping or breaking the false mirror. You can also use shiny stainless steel rather than mirrors. Nevertheless, if you want to keep it simple, just use the black cardboard.

# Rising Card

**THE MAGIC**: A card is freely chosen then returned to the deck. The magician chooses two other cards and slides them halfway into the deck. When the cards are pushed all the way into the deck, the chosen card slides out.

**THE MECHANICS**: Fan the deck and ask a spectator to pick a card, any card. They take the card out of the deck and look at it. Fan the deck again and have them insert it anywhere back into the deck. When the card is halfway in, bring the deck up so that the backs of the cards are facing the magician and the fronts are facing the spectators. Explain that you want everyone to see the card. You will be holding the fanned deck with both hands; the thumb of your left hand will bend the bottom left hand corner of the chosen card while you are showing the card to the audience. The bend does not have to be too much especially on a new deck. However, just enough for you to be able to locate the card once the deck is squared up.

Square up the deck and cut it a few times. Choose a card and look down towards the deck in your hand. Slide the card you just chose on one side of the bent card, putting it about halfway into the deck. Choose another card and slide it on the other side of the bent card about halfway into the deck, sandwiching it between the two cards.

Holding the deck with a slight amount of pressure, push these two cards up into the deck. As they move into the deck, the chosen card, the one with the bend, will rise out of the deck from the other end.

# Card through a Window

**THE MAGIC**: A card is selected and a corner is torn off and given to the spectator as a receipt to ensure that no switches will take place. The card is placed in the middle of the deck. One by one, the cards are counted, to show that there are only fifty-one cards, and the spectator's card is missing.

On a nearby window, the spectator's card is seen to have appeared, but stuck to the other side of the glass! The corner is held up to the card, and they match perfectly. Then, to offer a visual demonstration, another card is selected, and this time, the spectator signs it on the face. Again, the card is inserted into the middle of the deck and shuffled. Suddenly, the deck is thrown at an empty nearby window. After the cards have fallen, the signed card is seen to be stuck again on the other side of the glass.

The magician then proceeds to reach through the glass and pull their card out.

**THE MECHANICS**: Tear off one of the corners of a duplicate card and place it in your left pocket. Find a window near the area you are going to perform, and tape the card to the other side of it, with the face of the card facing where the spectators will be. Place the duplicate of that card in whatever position you like for your favorite force.

Also, smear a small amount of clear lip balm on the base of your left thumb, and keep a Sharpie handy.

First, you need to make sure that the planted card will be behind your audience, so they will not see it before it is time for the reveal. Begin by forcing the duplicate card via your favorite method. Have the spectator take the card. As they are doing this, secretly, reach into your left pocket and finger palm the torn corner. Now, tear a corner off their card and hold it in the fingers of your left hand. Bring your left hand up to hand them the corner for them to keep, and, as you do so, pull their corner into a classic palm, as you push forward and up on the duplicate corner, and give them the duplicate corner instead.

Take advantage of the misdirection of them examining the duplicate corner to slip the real corner into your pocket. Take the deck, and turn it face up. As you do this, secretly rub some of the lip balm from the base of your left thumb onto the back of the top card.

Place their card on the top of the deck, and give it a cut. The lip balm will cause the two cards to stick together, hiding the torn card. Count the cards, face up, into the hand of the spectator, showing only fifty-one cards and that the spectator's card has vanished. Draw attention to the window where the card is taped for the first reveal. Then, have another card freely selected and signed. Take the card, place it in the deck, and use your favorite method to control the card to the top.

After the card is on top, secretly smear the remaining lip balm across its back. Stand about four or five feet away from a window or glass door, and begin to throw the cards at it. You want to throw the first half of the deck as one solid block, and spring the second half, so it will force the signed card to stick to the window, but will give the appearance of randomness.

The card will appear to be stuck on the other side of the window. Walk up, and pretend to rub your hand over the glass, showing that it is really on the other side. Just keep your hand a few centimeters above the glass to avoid knocking it off. Then, without giving them time to inspect, cover the card partially with your left hand, reach up and grab a corner with your right hand, and slowly pull the card straight out of your hand, and towards yourself, giving the illusion that you are pulling it right through the glass.

# CHAPTER FIVE

## More Card Tricks

These tricks are the ones you can use to surprise and delight the crowd and can be performed in just about any setting. In this case, you never ask for a card to be chosen.

# Just as Much as You

**THE MAGIC**: The magician takes any deck of cards, even a borrowed deck, and places it on the table in front of his audience. A member of the audience is asked to take a few cards from the top of the deck and to secretly count how many he has. The magician takes some cards and does likewise. The magician then states, "I have just as many cards as you have, two more cards than you have, and enough to make you have a total of fourteen cards."

The magician asks the audience member how many cards he has and then proceeds to count off just as many cards as he has, two more cards and just enough left over to make the audience member's stack have exactly fourteen (as outlined in this example). It can be repeated frequently but the magician always makes it work.

I remember the late Doug Henning performing this trick on TV and it was such a great success that the magic stores were being inundated with requests to purchase this trick. Alas, such a trick was never available for sale. Nevertheless, here, for the first time is the secret.

**THE MECHANICS**: The secret of this trick is a quick math mind on the side of the magician. To start, when the audience member takes a few cards, you make certain you take a larger group of cards than he did. Watch him carefully since this is key to your success. Both of you count your cards, the magician mentally subtracts the amount of extra cards he wants to have from the number in his hand. The remainder becomes the amount you make the spectator end up with.

As an example, if the magician took nineteen cards and mentally subtracted three cards, the remainder would be sixteen. The magician would now state, "I have just as many cards as you have, three more cards than you have and enough cards left over to make you have sixteen." He would then ask, "How many cards do you have?"

It makes no difference how many cards are in the hands of the audience member, just as long as the magician made sure that he did not subtract too many cards to put him under the audience member's total number of cards. Suppose the audience member has eleven cards, the magician then proceeds, "I have just as many cards as you." Magician counts out eleven cards. "I have three more cards than you." Magician counts off three more cards. "And enough to make you have sixteen cards." Since in this case, the audience member replied that he had eleven cards, when the magician counts the remaining cards in his hand and adds that to the eleven in the audience member's hand, he will have sixteen.

Always do this trick two or three times, each with a different number of cards and it will fool them each time.

# Producing Cards from Thin Air

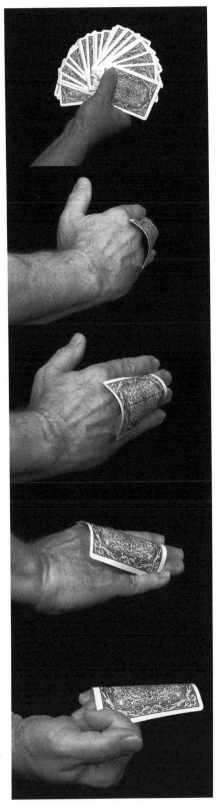

**THE MAGIC**: Cards appear from your empty hand.

**THE MECHANICS**: This can either be a trick on its own or it can be used in conjunction with any other card trick. This trick will take a great deal of practice, but in the end it will be well worth it.

Let's start by placing a single card in the first position. The card will be behind your hand, held in place by your fingers.

Picture one is how the hand looks to your audience.

To see how the card is held on the back of my hand, I will turn my hand halfway to reveal the secret.

In the third picture, I will turn my hand all the way over to show how the card is being held in place.

The edges of the card are between your fingers. When showing the trick, you begin by showing that your hand is empty. To make the card appear, you quickly bring your hand up and reach back with your thumb which will grab and snap the card into your hand.

This is an advanced, professional process and it will take work. Once you have it, you will be able to hide more cards. I know magicians who are able to hold twenty

cards in this manner and they can make them appear one at a time.

To get the card there in the first place, you can use your other hand or have someone place it there in order to begin the practice period required. Once you can make the move happen, placing the card there is a reversal of the process by starting with a card in your hand between your thumb and fingers.

# Cards from Your Mouth— A Harry Anderson Trick

**THE MAGIC**: After producing cards from the air one by one, you need a good finish. This is one great finish to back palming cards and producing them from thin air.

You point to your empty mouth and reach inside. Instantly a mouthful of cards pours out.

This is also a good finish to springing the cards from hand to hand.

This is another great fun trick that keeps the audience in a good mood.

**THE MECHANICS**: This trick is simple, although when you practice you will need to focus on the timing and misdirection involved.

Palm about twenty to thirty cards in your right hand. Leave this hand at your side. Do this when the attention is on something else, at the end of a previous trick, or after you have produced cards from thin air.

Point to your mouth with your left hand and open your eyes big.

As you start to open your mouth, bring your right hand up to your face and simply push the cards about halfway into your mouth. Immediately let the cards spill out and use your left hand to grab them as they come pouring out.

For your health's sake, do not use anyone else's cards for this. First, they do not want their cards in your mouth. More importantly, you do not know how many dirty and grimy hands have touched their cards. You do not want to make yourself sick.

# Magic Card in a Glass

**THE MAGIC**: The magician takes a drinking glass and announces that he is going to perform a card trick. In this unique trick, he will not touch the cards, because they will be inside the glass the whole time.

Placing the deck facing out in the glass, the magician states that he is going to find all four aces currently scattered throughout the deck using special "locator cards." He reaches into the glass, pulls out a card at random, and puts it in front of the rest of the cards in the deck so that it is the card the spectators now see through the drinking glass.

The magician then states that he will let that card serve as an ace. Holding the glass by the brim, the magician passes a cloth napkin quickly over the glass. When the napkin has completed its quick pass, the card in view in the glass has changed into an ace. The magician then takes the ace, puts it behind the deck within the glass, and passes the napkin over the glass a second time.

Again, the front card has been replaced with the ace. The same process is continued until all four aces have magically appeared in the glass.

**THE MECHANICS**: The preparation that is needed is a tall glass or a long-stemmed wine glass, so long as your deck of cards will stand within the glass. Many use only long-stemmed glasses, but it is not always needed. The glass must be clear and free of any markings, designs, etc.

Take the two red aces and glue them back-to-back. Do the same with the two black aces. Finally, glue two number cards back-to-back. In this example, we will use the six of spades and a red ten, glued back-to-back. We will also use the single six of clubs in the trick, and you will need an opaque napkin large enough to cover the glass.

Prepare the deck ahead of time by placing the six of clubs card face up on top of the facedown deck.

Now, set the double-sided black ace on top of it with the ace of spades showing. Next, place the six of spades/red ten card with the red ten face up and then the double-sided red aces. Finally, put the last red ten facedown on the facedown deck. You can use any cards you choose; I have chosen these cards in order to keep the instructions clear.

Here is how the cards are arranged on the bottom of the deck.

Square the card up and put them into a glass with the bottom card, any random card, facing the audience. Cover all with a napkin.

Announce that you are going to do the trick using a red locator card.

Uncover the glass and pull the red ten off the top of the deck and put it on the bottom, facing the spectator. This leaves the red ace facing the back of the glass, away from the audience. Holding the glass by the stem, you pass the napkin over the glass and spin it around so that a red ace is now facing the spectator. The napkin hides the glass when you spin it.

It helps if you hold the glass with your fingers rigid and the stem in the first bend of your finger. When you spin the glass, your thumb does the work and your fingers look pretty much the same. Now take the ace and put it on top of the deck.

The other side of the red ace pair is now on the bottom/back of the deck of cards. Cover the glass and perform the pass/spin again, and your spectator sees the other red ace. Now say that you need a black locator card. Take the red/black card off the top with the six facing and place it on the bottom, which is the side facing the audience. This leaves the black aces on the top of the deck. You want the ace of spades to be facing out on the top of the deck. When you cover and spin the glass again, the ace of spades is the black ace which will face the audience. You can ask the spectator to name a black ace. Nine out of ten times, they will say the ace of spades!

Cover the glass, spin it, and the ace of spades is there. You have made the chosen card appear for them.

If they happen to choose the ace of clubs, just say, "So that leaves the ace of spades," and make it appear.

# Acrobatic Aces

**THE MAGIC**: The four aces are dealt out with three random cards on each. The spectator is then asked to pick a pile and hold onto them. The magician magically commands the aces from the other piles to move to the stack being held by the spectator.

**THE MECHANICS**: Deal the four aces in a row so that the spectator can see them. Ask the spectator to name one of them. While the spectator deliberates, finger-break the top three cards of the deck.

Once the ace is chosen, put the other three aces facedown on top of the deck followed by the chosen card. Take the pile of aces along with the three hidden cards of the finger-break, from the top of the deck with your right hand. The aces should be face up with the selected ace on the top and the others and the three random cards below that. Make sure the spectator does not know about the three cards from the top of the deck. Square the pile of cards (four face-up aces and three facedown random cards). They should be held by the top and bottom edge, parallel to the deck that is still in the left-hand palm.

Slide off the top face-up ace and let it drop back onto the deck while flipping it over. This is done by drawing off the ace with the left thumb and flipping it with the edge of the cards in the right hand. Each ace, except for the last selected one, should in turn flip from right to left and end up facedown on the top of the deck. When turning over the last ace, the selected ace (with the three random cards) is dropped on top of the deck face up effectively placing three random cards between the selected ace and the three other aces. Continue in the following steps to turn over the ace and deal out the top four "aces" (the selected ace and three random cards).

The magician should say, "This is still your ace, correct?" showing the top card. The spectator will acknowledge it. Turn over the ace and proceed to deal out the four top cards (now the ace and three random cards). Follow up by saying, "I will now deal three random cards on each pile." You should now be dealing the three aces onto the chosen ace and random cards onto the other piles.

Square the piles and show only the first pile to prove that the original ace is still there (being careful not to flash the other aces).

Ask the spectator to place his hand on the stack of aces while you take the other stacks away. The magician explains, "Your pack has an ace and you want to keep it safe. These two packs," gesturing to two of the three packs, "have no owners so they do not need their aces." Make a motion that shows the spectator, in a magical way, that you are taking out the (non-existent) aces and throwing them to the spectator's pile. The magician continues, "Since you have three aces now and I only have one, I am sure to lose so I will just give you my ace." Pretend to throw your ace to his pile.

Turn over all three of the packs you have showing no aces. The spectator then turns his pile to discover that he has all the aces. This sort of trick, which appears to have occurred while the cards were in the control of the spectator, is nothing short of spectacular. Keep that in mind when you perform it. It is spectacular and you should be impressed with it.

# Full View Vanish

**THE MAGIC**: The magician shows the bottom card on the deck of cards. He passes his other hand in front of the card and the bottom card has changed.

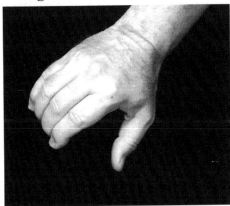

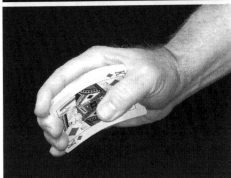

**THE MECHANICS**: Before showing the bottom of the deck, palm a few cards in your other hand. As the hand with the palmed cards meets the bottom of the deck, leave the palmed cards in place to cover the bottom card, but do not change the position of the hand, which was palming the cards. Keep it moving past the other hand and watch the faces of your spectators. They will see that the bottom card has changed and will think that you merely removed it with the other hand since that hand will now look suspicious as if you are hiding something. When you know you have their attention and have milked the trick enough, turn the hand over and show that it is empty. No need to say anything at this point. They will look back and forth between your hands and not get it.

Call attention to the deck of cards in your left hand. Your right hand with the palmed cards is at your right side. In one single smooth motion, pass your right hand over the left hand, pause for a moment when your hands meet; then continue to move your right hand down and away from your left hand.

Turn your right hand over, it is empty and return your attention to your left hand where the bottom card has changed. The old bottom card is buried several cards into the deck. Sometimes showing a few of the bottom cards is good showmanship too.

# Magic Lesson

**THE MAGIC**: The magician asks the spectator whether he knows any card tricks. Whatever the spectator answers, the magician continues by saying, "Well, here is a great trick. I will teach you to perform."

The spectator is handed a deck of cards and is asked to hold them with the cards facing the magician and the backs toward the spectator. The magician picks a card, which the spectator removes and places on the table, never looking at it.

The spectator, after mixing the cards, ends up with two piles of cards on the table. The top cards on each pile are turned over, and one reveals the value of the selected card while the other reveals the suit.

**THE MECHANICS**: The key to this trick is presentation and the fact that the magician never actually handles the deck.

After the spectator shuffles the deck, have him fan them in front of his face with the backs of the cards towards himself. Tell him to start fanning at the top of the deck and continue to the bottom. Meanwhile, you watch for a card that has the same value as the top card and the same suit as the card second from top. Be careful that the two cards you choose do not have the same value or the same suit as each other or the trick will not work. If this is not the case, ask the spectator to mix up the deck and fan again.

When you find that particular card, touch it and have him pull it out and place it on the table facedown. Then tell him to think of a number and to count that many cards into a neat pile facedown on the table. This puts the two pointer cards on the bottom of the pile.

Have him discard the rest of the cards in his hands, pick up the pile on the table, and deal the cards alternately into two facedown piles. The two pointer cards are now on top of each of the new piles. Remember that the last card he deals will show the value (ace, two, three, etc) of the selected card while the next-to-last card, the top one on the other pile, will show the suit.

Explain to the spectator that if he has been concentrating on the card on the table, he will have subconsciously picked two cards that will respectively reveal the value and suit of the card that you the magician have randomly selected. Flip the three cards to reveal that this is so.

That is it, school's out.

# Wallet Locator

**THE MAGIC**: Hand the deck to a spectator, have him shuffle and mix the cards, then randomly deal the cards out haphazardly onto and all over the table. The magician drops his wallet onto the cards when the spectator is done. Spectator opens the wallet, reads the note, and removes the deck to reveal the card below the wallet is the one predicted in the note.

**THE MECHANICS**: Remove one card, such as the queen of diamonds or any card of your choice. Write a note stating the queen of diamonds will be found below the wallet. Place both into your pocket.

Hand the deck of cards to the spectator and ask them to shuffle them, then deal them onto the table until all the cards are used up and are scattered all over the table. You can ask them to slide them all around after they are done dealing in order to ensure a large mix of cards.

When they are done and the cards are well strewn across the table, remove your wallet and the queen. The queen should be facedown and unseen under your wallet. Drop your wallet onto the mess of cards.

With the spectator watching, open the wallet to reveal the note, ask that the note be removed, opened, and read. They are to then follow the instructions. The instructions will say, *lift the wallet and turn over the card directly below the wallet to reveal the queen of diamonds.*

# My Friend Flicka

**THE MAGIC**: The magician places a playing card on the tip of his index finger, balancing it. On top of the card, he places a coin; now both are being balanced. He asks the spectator to do the same thing with his own hand. The magician challenges the spectator to remove the card but leave the coin resting on the fingertip. When the spectator fails, the magician prevails.

**THE MECHANICS**: You need just one card from a new pack of cards and a coin of your choice; a quarter works well.

The coin must be exactly in place over the inside tip of your finger, right above the finger print area.

With the card and coin balanced on your left-hand index finger, flick your right-hand index finger from under and up against the edge of one end of the card, striking the card with a hard snap of your finger.

The card should fly away from your finger leaving the coin in place, balancing on your fingertip.

Snapping the card with your other hand takes a little practice but once perfected you have a perfect trick. Most spectators will try to pull the card out quickly like the old tablecloth pulling trick. It will not work; only a quick flick from your other hand will do the job.

# Card from Tumbler Vanish

**THE MAGIC:** The magician causes a card to vanish from a glass tumbler being held by the spectator.

**THE MECHANICS:** You need a deck of cards, a glass tumbler, and a piece of plastic cut to the exact size as a playing card. Stiff, clear sheets of plastic can be found at an arts and crafts store. Buy a single sheet and cut it to the same size as a playing card. For the performance, you will also need a handkerchief, cloth, or towel large enough to completely cover the tumbler. The glass tumbler should be taller than a playing card and wide enough at the top to admit a card. It should taper towards the bottom, and, by preference, be ornamented; that will help hide the clear plastic card you will have placed into it.

Choose a face card and carefully bend it in half. Straighten it out and place it on the top of the deck with the clear plastic card on top of it. This card now has a crease where you have previously bent it.

The tumbler stands on the table, also a deck of cards with the creased card on top and the piece of plastic beneath it.

Someone is asked to assist and he is allowed to examine the glass, which he is told to hold up with his right hand.

The magician picks up the creased card with his right hand and with it the plastic, which is kept concealed behind it. The spectator is asked to call out the name of the card. The magician holds the card with his thumb at the bottom and his forefinger at the top, bending it out a little to keep the plastic card in place. Then with his left hand, the magician takes the handkerchief, places it over the card, and asks the spectator to place the tumbler under it. As soon as the card is covered, the magician takes hold of it through the handkerchief with his left hand, while the right hand, which is still under the handkerchief, bends the card in two and palms it. Since it is only half size now, it should be palmed without being detected. The left hand holds on to the plastic card, its outline under the handkerchief gives the impression that the card is still there. The spectator is requested to take hold of the card (the plastic card) from outside the handkerchief.

"Please take hold of the handkerchief and the card," asks the magician. The spectator is asked to push the card into the tumbler, which is still covered. The magician gets rid of the palmed card by dropping it into a pocket while digging into the pocket for magic, invisible vanishing powder. The magician then informs the spectator that the card will leave the tumbler in a moment, without his knowing it.

Pulling up his sleeves, the magician puts his left hand under the handkerchief and grasps the glass near the bottom, telling the spectator to let go of it. At the same moment catching hold of a corner of the handkerchief, the magician jerks away the handkerchief away, showing that the tumbler is empty. It may be turned around since the clear plastic will not be seen. The tapering sides of the glass will hold the plastic card firmly, which is curled slightly inside the lower part of the tumbler. The design traced on the tumbler helps in the deception and effectually conceals the plastic card.

# David Blaine Card Miracle

**THE MAGIC**: David Blaine has made this trick very popular. He shows the spectator a card, the queen of hearts, for example. He places it, facedown, into the spectator's hand, and asks the person to sandwich the card between both hands.

He then shows the next card, the king of diamonds, and rubs it facedown over the sandwiched card, but when he turns it over, the audience is amazed to see that the card is now the queen of hearts and the sandwiched card has become the king of diamonds. The two cards seemed to have changed places right before your eyes.

**THE MECHANICS**: The setup is very simple, as you just need to prepare two identical cards. In our case, we are using two kings of diamonds.

On the top of the deck, the top three cards should be the king of diamonds, queen of hearts, and the duplicate king of diamonds. It does not matter about the order of the rest of the deck as only the first three are used.

Ask the spectator to extend their hand. At the same time, perform a double flip card control move with the top two cards. The spectator will be looking at the queen of hearts, but you will actually be holding the queen with the king of diamonds behind it.

Ask the spectator to name the card being displayed by you. When named, turn double over again so that the cards are facedown with the king of diamonds on top of the deck. Place the top card onto the spectator's outstretched hand.

It will be assumed that you placed the queen onto the outstretched hand, when it was the king.

Ask the spectator then to place the other hand over the card to sandwich it between both hands. Then ask whether the sandwiched card is still remembered. Remind them that the queen is still in their hand.

Double flip card control the top two cards while the spectator is still sandwiching a card between both hands. The spectator will be looking at the king, but you will have the queen card with the king hiding it. Ask the spectator to name the card in your hand.

Place the double back on top of the deck again. Remove the top card. The spectator will think it is the king when it is really the queen. Then rub this card over the sandwiched hands. After doing this ask, "Did you feel anything?"

The spectator may be confused, but when the card is revealed and shown to be the one thought to be in the sandwiched hand, this person will be frankly amazed. Then the spectator looks at the card, which was sandwiched between both hands, and once again is amazed, as this is the king.

# The Sucker Aces

**THE MAGIC**: The four aces are shown on the bottom of the deck, but the spectators are not fooled. They see that they are not aces, they see that they are actually threes. The magician tells the spectators that he will do magic and changes these aces into other cards.

The spectators will not stand for the deception and voice their opposition to the trick by shouting out that they see the cards are not aces at all and the trick will not fool them. The magician will act bewildered, even disappointed. Since the spectators are so smart and do not like the trick, then so be it. The magician gives up, but before he does, he turns over the four cards and, to the spectator's amazement, they are the four aces.

**THE MECHANICS**: Stack the bottom of the deck with an ace, a three, an ace, a three, etc. until all four aces and all four threes are on the bottom of the deck. The bottom card will be a three, then an ace, and so on. The last three should be the three of spades since most know that the ace of spades is usually a very ornamental card.

To make the trick work, you will need to do a bottom glide (see page 29).

Show the bottom card of the deck and cover the top and bottom pip, or symbol, on the three with both of your hands. Announce that this is the ace of so-and-so and that you will change it to another card. All the spectator will see is the middle pip of the card and they will doubt what they are looking at. Face the deck down, do a bottom glide, place the ace on the table, and move the bottom card, the three, to the top of the deck. Do not offer an explanation for this move or draw attention to it. Bring the deck back up and show the next three, again covered by your fingers. Continue to do this until all four threes have been shown as you continue to tell the spectators they are looking at aces and you will make them change to different cards. By the time you get to the last three, the three of spades, the spectators should have caught on that they are not looking at aces but at threes.

Notice their obvious disappointment in the trick and play with it. Joke back and forth with them as you casually mix the deck.

When you are done, tell them that the trick is ruined and that you will not bother changing the aces into anything else, and turn them over to show the aces are still there. This will lead to a great deal of astonishment by the spectators who will wonder what happened to the threes.

# Ace to Three

**THE MAGIC**: The magician turns an ace to a three right before the spectator's eyes.

**THE MECHANICS**: Place the ace of diamonds on top of the deck and the three of diamonds at the bottom. To begin the trick, the magician gives the ace of diamonds to a spectator. Cut the deck and place the bottom half on top. The three will be the bottom card of the top section of the deck. When the deck is closed, the magician separates the two halves of the deck by inserting between the little finger of the left hand that is holding the deck.

Open the deck at the place of the original separation and ask the spectator to replace the card in the deck. When the ace is replaced, it should be directly under the three. Putting his little finger between the ace and the three, the magician makes the pass, bringing these cards to their original position on top and at the bottom of the deck. "Now," says the magician, "I will dispatch the ace on its travels, by sending it from the middle of the deck to the bottom." He riffles the deck and shows the ace, apparently, at the bottom.

What he really does is hold the deck at its ends by both hands, the fingers covering the end spots of the three making it look like an ace. Then he covers the face of the cards with his left hand and presses the deck against his forehead. With his other hand, he strikes the hand that holds the deck. This, he says, is to drive the ace through the deck. He removes the deck from his forehead and the ace is seen

sticking there. This is affected by having the forehead dampened before beginning the trick or by wetting the back of the card with a little spittle.

Removing the ace from his forehead, the magician spins it through the air. You can spin it by grabbing a corner of the card and throw it up into the air. The card spins, and as it falls, it is evident that it really is the ace of diamonds. The magician catches it and says, "Now watch it," and once more sets it spinning through the air. Everyone can see that it is the ace. This time as it comes down, the magician does not touch it, but allows it to reach the ground. "Will someone," he asks, "be good enough to pick it up, and tell us what card it is." Moreover, to the surprise of all it proves to be the three.

The secret of the second part of this trick is that after the magician catches the flying ace, he returns it to top of the deck. When it is time to spin the card again, he takes the three from the bottom of the deck instead of the ace off the top of the deck. When the card is spun in the air, people cannot seem to tell if it is a three or an ace because of the fast spinning motion. The end spots of the three seeming to be drawn into the center spot making it look like an ace when it is spinning.

# Locate All Four Aces

**THE MAGIC**: The magician hands out the deck and asks that it be thoroughly shuffled, and then placed in his pocket. The magician reaches into his pocket and removes the four aces.

**THE MECHANICS**: Before handing out the deck, secretly remove the four aces and place them in your pocket. Once the deck has been shuffled and placed into your pocket, reach in and remove the top four cards; these are the aces previously secreted away into your pocket.

Another variation would have a spectator shuffle the deck and the magician would take the deck and put it into his pocket along with the aces that are already there. The deck goes in on top of the four aces, with all the cards facing in the same direction. The four aces end up facedown on the top of the deck in your pocket.

The magician will ask the spectator to call out a number between one and ten. When you draw the cards out of your pocket, count the first number from the bottom of the deck and then take the "next" card from the top. You repeat this three times. When you turn over the top cards of the four separate piles on the table, they are all aces.

With this trick, you are proving that you can "force" the spectator to locate the aces by finding their position in the deck. That is why the spectator is calling out a number between one and ten. The next card after each location in the deck just happens to be an ace.

# CHAPTER SIX

## Bonus Magic Tricks

Here are some of my favorite tricks, and although you might recognize them from other publications, I have taken the liberty to update and more specifically define them just for you, my very favorite friends.

# Bags of Cards

**THE MAGIC**: The magician hands several paper bags (usually five) to members of the audience. Before doing so, he shows the audience that an ace of spades has been inserted into one of the bags; the other four each has one of the kings. The bags are mixed. The magician concentrates, and then asks the volunteers to set fire to two of the bags and return to their seats with the other two. One bag remains on stage. The ace of spades is found in the bag remaining on the stage.

**THE MECHANICS**: Simplicity is the key to this trick, along with great stage presence and presentation. The ace of spades is never placed into any of the bags. Instead, the magician pretends to put it in. The ace has, in fact been concealed in the magician's palm during the process of pretending to place it into the bag.

At the end of the trick, the magician takes hold of the remaining bag and violently tears it open while the palmed card seems to mysteriously emerge from the torn bag.

I have also seen this effect done in a comedy motif, where the magician will borrow a high-denomination bill from someone in the audience. During the trick, the magician will make out as if the trick has not worked. He does this by tearing open the last bag and pretending to find no money within. Then the magician asks the spectator who helped him before to now open their bags, search their pockets, and even look under their seats. Still no money.

At this point, the audience believes the money has literally gone up in smoke, only to have the magician recover the money from a pocket or behind an ear.

This effect works as above, except the money does not have to be palmed when the onstage bag is opened. A good way to get rid of the palmed money is to reach into a pocket for matches used in burning the stage bags.

Rather than burning the bags, you can have all five bags mixed by the audience members, and then send them back to their seats. Take each bag, one at a time and tear them to pieces until only one bag is left. This will be the bag with the ace inside.

# Watch the Watch

**THE MAGIC:** The magician will use a wristwatch to correctly guess the secretly chosen number of a spectator.

**THE MECHANICS:** Show a watch and ask someone to think of any number from one to twelve. Tap a pencil against the numbers of the watch dial. As you do this, tell the spectator to mentally count to twenty, once for each tap, beginning with one above the number they are thinking of. Make the first seven taps anywhere on the watch face. On the eighth, tap your pencil on the number twelve. Continue tapping the numbers counterclockwise around the dial. When the spectator reaches twenty,

your pencil will be pointing to the number he is thinking of.

Let's pretend that the spectator has secretly chosen the number six. Tap the watch twenty times. On the twentieth tap, you end up on the number six.

When presenting the trick, the magician asks a member of the audience to think of a number between one and twelve. "Don't tell me the number," the magician says, "just think of it. Got it, good. I will tap the numbers on my watch. Beginning with the first tap, begin counting to twenty in your head. When you reach twenty say stop. When you say stop, the last number I tapped will be your secretly chosen number. Ready to begin? On my first tap, begin counting with the number one higher than the one you have chosen and keep counting until you reach twenty."

"If I pick the number three," the audience member might ask, "I begin by counting four on your first tap."

"Yes," you tell them.

Begin to tap; they count quietly in their head. When they reach twenty they shout "stop" and magically, you have reached their secretly chosen number. It is mathematical and works every time.

# The Card House Illusion

**THE MAGIC**: The magician enters the stage area carrying a part of the card house (see illustrations below). The house is in three sections: the roof, the front and a side section, and the back with a side section. The three pieces each look like giant playing cards. Each piece will be picked up by the magician and shown inside and out. The magician puts the parts together, forming a card house. The completed house will be three feet tall

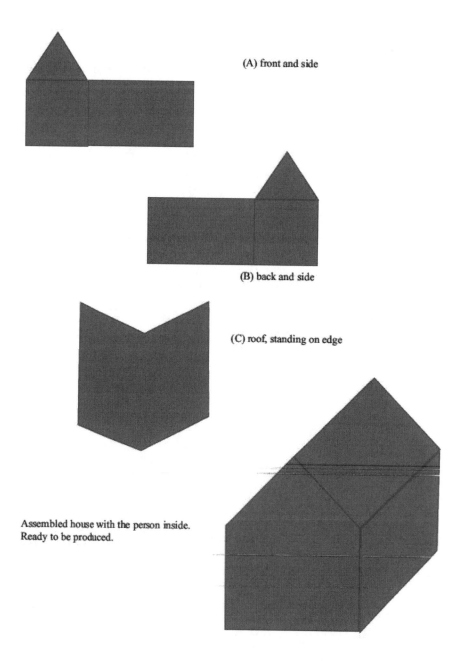

(A) front and side

(B) back and side

(C) roof, standing on edge

Assembled house with the person inside.
Ready to be produced.

(at the peak of the roof), two feet wide (the front of the house), and three feet deep (the length of the sides).

Once the house has been assembled, it can be pushed around as a completed unit to show that there is no funny business going on. At the magician's command, the roof pops off the house and out steps one or two assistants depending on the magician's wishes. No trap doors or special stage settings are required for this effect.

**THE MECHANICS**: This effect takes timing and coordination from both the magician and those who are to be magically produced. When the magician enters the stage with the first part of the card house, the other two parts are already on the stage, standing flat to one side. The roof is standing on its end so that the roof peak is facing the audience. In this position, an assistant will be hiding behind the roof but would be unseen by the audience because they are behind the roof. Make sure the roof peak is next to a stage curtain. In this manner, the assistant who will be made to appear can crawl from backstage, behind the curtain and then continue, unseen, behind the roof. If the stage does not have curtains or wings, have the roof section standing near anything that will conceal your assistant with enough cover that someone could crawl from the hiding space behind the roof without being seen.

The backside section is leaning flat up against the peaked roof section. The section carried by the magician is the front-side section.

As an alternative, you can drag the roof out, while the person crawls along behind the roof, hidden. Then go back for the next piece and lean it against the roof. Finally, return with the next and last piece of the house.

With the three pieces all on stage, the magician opens the front-side section. The magician shows it front and back, and then sets it up just next to the roof section. Then the magician picks up the backside section, shows it all around, and then places this part next to the front-side section. The magician begins to hook the front section to the side section. At this point, there will be space between the end section and the house for those who will be produced to crawl into the house unseen. Once the front of the house has been connected and the people have crawled into the house, the magician walks to the rear of the house for the final hookup. Then the magician picks up the roof, shows it all around, and then places it upon the house. The house now is fully assembled.

In this position, the assistant(s) to be produced are safely concealed in the house.

For the most part, the subterfuge is complete. The magician can shift the house to the center of the stage and spin it around. In moving the house, magician must be careful not to move quickly, since the house occupants must crawl along at the same speed.

Remember: When spinning the house around, make sure you spin the house without moving it from its center spot. This way the hidden assistant or assistants can remain in one spot while the house spins around them.

When it is time to produce the person or people, the magician can tap on the house. The assistants within only have to stand up. They will lift the roof off the house as they stand. The roof will fly off, back over the rear of the house and out of the way, usually falling flat onto the stage. The magician then disconnects the front of the house so the assistants can walk out onto the stage. This action will also reveal that the house is now empty.

This illusion is simply constructed and can be performed by the raw beginner, as well as the most accomplished professional. Corrugated cardboard can be used for the house material. Tape can be used to connect the sections together. An elastic band on the front and another at the back can be used to connect the front side and backside sections together during the performance. The roof section simply sits or rests on the top of the assembled house.

This illusion may sound like a simple effect, but astonishes audiences when done with the great showmanship and flair.

I used this illusion to produce a panther along with its handler on television and used the same trick at large arenas to produce people, tigers, lions, and once, even produced a bear. Oh my!

# Magical Moving Pencil

**THE MAGIC**: A pencil moves across the table or bar top as the magician seemingly uses his mind power to move it.

**THE MECHANICS**: Place an unlit pencil (a straw can also be used) on a flat surface such as a counter or bar. Explain to the onlookers that you are able to move this pencil using telekinesis. Move your hands back and forth over the object as if you are commanding it to move. Signal with your palm for the pencil to move away from you. The signal is whatever pleases you and it should be some sort of movement that seems to be magical. Ham it up. Secretly, lightly blow at the object to push it and it will move.

You can also make the pencil roll towards you if you cup your palm behind the object and blow into your palm. Your breath will reflect off of your cupped hand and push the pencil towards you. Remember, it's not what you do and no matter how corny it might look, if you do it right it will surprise and fool your audience.

# Circle, Card, Square

**THE MAGIC**: This trick is a basic principle of magic. The methodology can be used for many different effects, both close up and onstage and it is closely related to the Card House Illusion (see page 85).

The magician shows a large square box with four sides, each side depicting a playing card. The square has neither a top nor a bottom. It is held up to the audience and they can see right through the opening. Next the magician shows a cylinder-shaped box (the circle), which also has neither a top nor a bottom; it, too, is shown to be empty by holding it up to the audience and looking through it. The circle has a greater circumference than the square and it can be placed over the square. Then with a flourish and with the right word, out pops an assistant.

**THE MECHANICS**: This trick can be made small for close-up or large enough for a stage production with an assistant. You can make objects or people appear or disappear, depending only upon the size of the circle and square. The trick is made up of a cylinder and a box. The cylinder is large enough to fit over the box, completely covering it. Neither box nor cylinder has a top or bottom. The cylinder and the box are not faked. In the simplest form, the person or object, which is going to appear, is in the cylinder, which begins on a table or the middle of the stage (depending on the size of the illusion). The box is shown to be empty; it is then placed into the cylinder. Then the cylinder is lifted and shown to be empty. Now the person or object is hidden by the box. When the cylinder is replaced over the box, the tricky part is done. From the audience's point of view, you have shown both box and cylinder to be empty. It is not what you do as a magician, it is how you do it. You don't say you will make something appear. You don't say that nothing is hidden. All you do is show the circle and the square. What happens at the end when you produce something from nothing is the entire effect.

In a variation of the same trick, you can enhance the effect by cutting a "window," which is simply an opening into the box. Without bringing too much attention to this fact, remove the brightly colored cylinder (if this is how you have decorated it) from over the box. The window will now show what appears to be the inside of the box. Then replace the cylinder and lift the box. Both were shown empty. So where was the person or object? There is an inner cylinder (inside the box), which the audience does not and cannot see since it is always inside either the box or the square. It is smaller in diameter than the colored cylinder and it is painted flat black, the same color as the inside of both the box and the colored cylinder.

When the audience looks through the window after the colored cylinder has been removed, they are looking at the exterior or the inner cylinder and not the inside of the box. When done in this version, the illusion can be viewed in the round without having any trouble spots for the magician. In fact, even easier, the person in the box will hold up a black bit of cardboard larger than the window. This will conceal the person in the box and appear to show an empty box. Fooling people is easy because the audience does not know what will happen. All they see is a window that seems to be showing the contents to be empty.

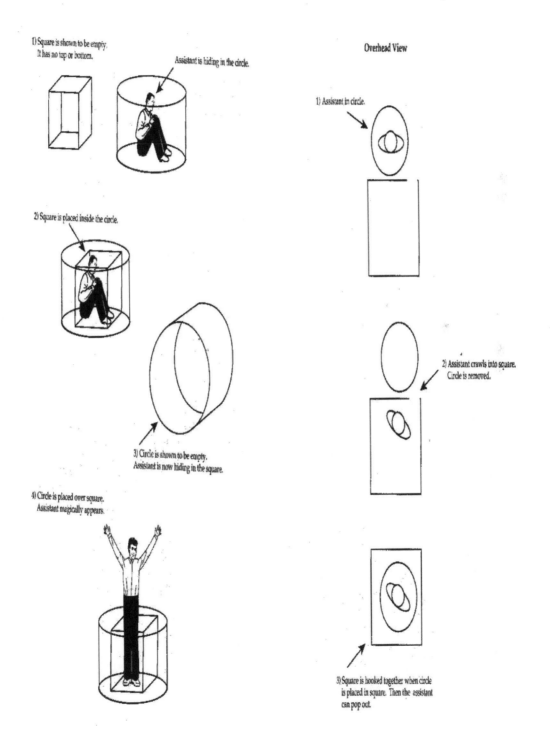

1) Square is shown to be empty. It has no top or bottom.

Assistant is hiding in the circle.

2) Square is placed inside the circle.

3) Circle is shown to be empty. Assistant is now hiding in the square.

4) Circle is placed over square. Assistant magically appears.

**Overhead View**

1) Assistant in circle.

2) Assistant crawls into square. Circle is removed.

3) Square is hooked together when circle is placed in square. Then the assistant can pop out.

Another concept is to have the square fit over the cylinder rather than vice versa. In this arrangement, you would make the inner hiding place a square rather than a circle.

A third option is to perform this effect like that of the Card House Illusion. Only one cylinder and one box or square is used. The person is hidden in the cylinder, which is placed behind the square. The square is not attached on all sides; in fact, the back and one side are open and ajar. When you begin, you lift the square and show it to be empty. When you replace it to the stage, you place it directly in front of the circle. The back of the square is open. When you lift the circle, the assistant crawls into the square from their hiding place inside of the circle. Then you place the circle into the square and over the appeared. Spin the box around and hook up the back and side. Then out pops the assistant.

If the illusion is made for table size, you can produce a rabbit or scarfs or any number of items.

# Dinner Prediction

**THE MAGIC**: You are out to dinner with friends. After they have looked at the menu, but before they announce their choices, you ask them each a few personal questions, about their hobbies, incomes, and love lives. Anything you are feeling interested about. You claim their answers contain psychological clues about what your friends feel like eating.

You write down a prediction for each person, fold it up, and isolate it in the middle of the table. The guests place their orders. Now it time for the magic. Call over the waiter and ask him to read out what you have written.

Your guesses are all correct. Your friends look at you uneasily, afraid you may know them too well. Or they simply enjoy the show of prestidigitation.

**THE MECHANICS**: This has been adapted from a fraud that "psychic readers" used to get information about their clients' dead relatives. Nevertheless, do not worry; the only special skill it requires is the ability to look your friends straight in the eye and fib.

The first step of this trick is pure espionage. Before you arrive at the table, you must find out what one of your fellow diners is going to order.

You may already know what somebody usually eats, if you were having lunch with your mother, for example, and you know that she loves turkey, you could count on her ordering turkey.

There are other ways to determine what someone will order. On the way to the restaurant, for example, you could influence somebody's choice by raving about a certain dish. When the waiter is naming the daily specials, you could see if anyone nods and immediately closes the menu.

You may just want to let your date or buddy in on the gag and prearrange for them to order a particular dish.

The second step: you arrive at the restaurant, sit down with your group, and lead the conversation around to the trick. For example, you might say, "Has anybody here read *We Are What We Eat and We Eat What We Do*? They won't have, it does not exist, but it sounds like the title of an airport book put out by some publisher. Therefore, they keep listening.

"It tells how certain activities cause certain food cravings. It certainly makes sense that playing tennis and reading *Wild Wild West* leave you hungry for different things."

It does not make sense, but they probably will not contradict you. At dinner, it's considered rude to say, "That is rubbish. Prove it!" Even if what the person is saying is transparently silly. Etiquette gives cranks the advantage, so play the role of a crank.

Continue: "I've gotten really good at guessing what people are going to order. All I have to do is ask you a couple of questions. Want to try it?" They do; they expect you to make a fool of yourself.

Then you can say, "Okay, look over the menu and decide what you want. When you are sure, close the menu and do not tell anyone what you have chosen.

Take out a little pad of paper and hold it so no one can see the page you are writing on. This is very important; in fact, the whole trick hinges on it because you will never be writing what the audience thinks you are writing.

Let us imagine you are doing this trick for your friends John, Barbie, Brian, and Dovid, and that you have done your espionage homework on Dovid and found out she will be ordering corned beef and cabbage.

Begin by picking any of the diners except Dovid. Let us start with John.

Ask John a few questions about his life (e.g., what time he gets up, how his boss is treating him, etc.). It doesn't matter what you ask, as long as you pretend each of his answers is giving you clues about his food preferences.

Everyone thinks you are writing down what you think John will order for dinner. But they're wrong, actually, you write: Dovid—corned beef and cabbage.

Don't let anyone see what you have written! Fold up the little paper and toss it in the middle of the table (it's more dramatic if you can isolate it in, say, an unused glass, dish or tray).

Now you say, while pointing to the folded paper, "Okay, there's my prediction, John. I won't touch it again. So now you can tell us, what are you going to have?"

Whatever John tells you, memorize it and nod your head.

You now ask Barbie the same questions or any other hair-brained questions you choose and pretend to write your thoughts on Barbie. In fact, you are writing what John told you he wanted for his meal.

Again, do not let anyone see what you have written. Fold up the little paper and toss it in the middle of the table.

Now you say to Barbie, "Okay, there's my prediction, Barbie. I won't touch it again. So now you can tell us, what are you going to have?"

Continue the swindle with Brian. When you reach Dovid, you write what Brian has told you he wants as his meal.

You are done.

Four guests, four predictions, and you got them all right.

Hand the four slips of paper to the waiter and wait for the reaction.

# Zigzag

**THE MAGIC**: Doug Henning popularized this illusion in the early 1970s when he began touring. Doug and I were good friends and had a friendly rivalry going on as well. We both started our careers in Toronto and had a blast along the way.

In the illusion, a tall box the height of the magician's assistant is wheeled to center stage. The box is visibly in three equal sections. The drawing of a young lady is depicted on the outside of the box, with openings cut out at the level of her face, hands, and right foot. Small doors are located on the front of each section.

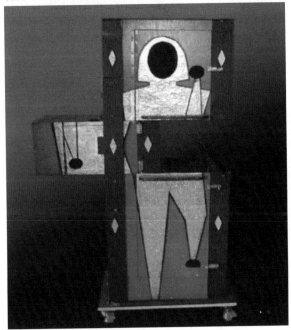

**THE MECHANICS**: When all three doors are open, the entire box can be clearly seen as being empty. Through the open doors steps the assistant. The doors are closed upon the entry of the assistant but the audience can clearly see her whole face through the top door's small opening. She also extends her hands through the hand holes in the top box and her toes through the foot holes in the bottom box. Wide steel blades are then inserted, into the front and pushed to the back. One blade is inserted between the first and second box section. Then another blade is inserted between the second and third box section.

The assistant appears to be cut into three equal pieces. To make this illusion even more amazing, the magician slides the middle section completely to the right of the assistant. All the while, the face, hands, and foot of the assistant continue to be completely visible to the audience.

The secret is that this trick is more of an optical illusion than anything else. Yes, the assistant's hands, foot, and face are real. It is the box that is strangely built. When the middle section, or box, is moved to the right of the assistant, a special section of the box moves with it. This special section is an extended part of the box. The box looks like it moves completely to the right, when in fact it only moves about five inches to the right.

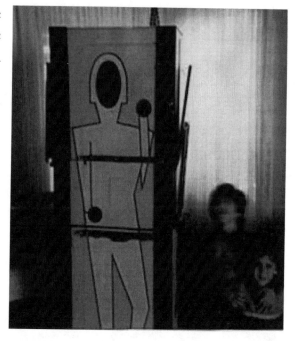

The edges of the box are painted black; this border color hides the fact that the box has not moved that much. The assistant is curled around the blades and the middle box. Although from the view of the audience such a position is impossible, for the assistant the task is easy, although not comfortable.

The real point of the blades is to hide the inside of the boxes from the audience. The moveable box has a layer of black cloth material on the top and bottom of its section. This material moves along with the box, hiding the insides of the box and hiding the secret.

The uniqueness of this illusion is not so much how it works, but the fact that it can be done in the round meaning that it is angle proof. It is easy to use, easy to move, and can be performed quickly and magically at just about any theatre or stage setting.

The entire illusion is on casters, which allows for turning the illusion around to all sides both before, during, and after the trick has been performed adding considerably to the confusion and amazement of the audience.

Don't let the simplicity of this illusion turn you off. It is a great illusion that has done marvelous things for magician's careers. Many magicians add a change of clothes to this illusion. The assistant goes into the box in an evening gown and comes out in a bathing suit. Sometimes it is the magician who goes into the box and has the trick done to him by his assistant.

The two young men are two of my five sons, Adam and Brian; thanks guys.

# Giant Three-Card Monte

Stage-sized magic tricks on a budget is not a contradiction. The following stage-sized trick can be constructed for less than a hundred dollars and it plays very big to an audience. I discuss this trick in the introduction as to how charlatans use a small version of this process to cheat money out of people. In this stage-sized version, the only outcome is magic.

The Background: Three Card Monte is a con game played on the streets of Manhattan, Madrid, Mexico, and other big cities around the world. In the street version, the dealer will show three cards, mix them up, and ask that you follow one of the cards with your eyes. He will have you bet on the card and let you win until the betting gets out of hand. Then he will keep you losing until you have lost all of your money. In our stage version, no betting is involved and the outcome is a good surprise and not a ripoff.

**THE MAGIC**: Three cards are moved about on the stage. Each is six feet tall and three feet wide. The cards are moved all around, spun around, and then formed into a triangle from which emerges the magician's assistant or the magician himself.

**THE MECHANICS**: First, you need to build the illusion. If you are on a budget, I suggest building the frame for each card from soft, light pine. Cover the pine with a white sheet. Spray paint each white sheet with the likeness of a playing card. Two queen cards and one king card will be good for the three card panels. Be certain to use either enough paint to make the sheets opaque or use sheets, which are themselves opaque.

Because each card will need to be moved about, a minimum of four people will be needed for this trick. Three will control the three cards and the fourth person will make the magical appearance. The cards are never lifted off the stage but are dragged about, upright.

The trick begins when the three cards are dragged upright onto the stage. The cards each face the audience and as the trick progresses, the cards are all moved about the stage, turned around and eventually formed into a triangle. The trick is to keep the person who will make the magical appearance behind one of the cards at all times and unseen by the audience.

This is easier said than done and much practice is needed to coordinate the hiding of the person as the cards are moved about the stage. Careful choreography and timing is needed.

Although there is no set pattern since the amount of time, size of stage, and angles to the audience must all play a part in the scheme, it is something to work out and rehearse in order to get it right.

The cards are wide enough to keep the appearance person hidden while the one who is moving the card keeps it all together.

To begin the presentation of this trick, talk about Three Card Monte and tell the audience to keep their eyes on the odd card (which in this scenario is the king card). Use your imagination and keep the audience thinking that you are talking about Three Card Monte. It's all part of the deception; the most important thing is not to give away the ending.

When you form the cards up, leave the odd card, the king card, as the back of your triangle. Ask the audience, "Where is the king? On the back of the triangle, right?"

As the cards pass each other on the stage, the appearance person can secretly move from behind one card to another. Once you have exhausted the audience and proven that the cards are not hiding anything, form the triangle of cards with the first card facing the audience; this will be the card currently hiding the assistant. Rotate the entire triangle around in a circle until a point of two cards faces the audience.

Separate the point and out walks your assistant. Explain to the audience that this shows how easy it is to be fooled and never bet with a street urchin.

# CHAPTER SEVEN

## Why You Should Do Tricks with Cards

Once you know the "how to" part, which you have learned earlier in this book, you should also understand the "why" of performing magic with cards.

Cards are mostly well known to people. They know there are four sets; diamonds, clubs, hearts, and spades. They know that each set has thirteen cards and they know that some cards are number cards and some are face cards. They also know about joker cards in a deck. Being so well-known makes them less suspicious to the general public. When magical apparatuses such as boxes or other odd items are used, they are unknown to most people and it raises their suspicion. Cards are also user-friendly because they come in a card box and fit in your pocket. Most of the tricks in this book are with a standard deck of cards and can be performed with the magician's deck or a borrowed deck. All of this adds to the ease of the performance.

When I first began using cards for making magic, I was only seven years old. The cards were so big compared to my small hands that it was a great challenge to perform even the simplest of magic tricks. I was determined to learn magic and be able to fool my family and my friends. I never gave up and kept on practicing until my hands would grow stiff and sore. My first audience was my mother and she would watch patiently as I tried trick after trick on her. As a loving mother, she was awestruck by each and every miracle I performed. I did not get the same results from my two older sisters; both were quick to point out my mistakes and misgivings. Still, I persevered and refused to quit, spending hours in front of a mirror my dad set up in my room for me to practice in front of. Finally the day came when my older sisters would say, how did you do that? It was then that I realized that knowing how to do a trick was nothing compared to performing it properly.

# The History of Cards

From what I have researched, playing cards originated sometime before 1200 AD in China and were introduced into Europe after the thirteenth century.

Lut Chi was the main type of playing cards and the oldest reference to a deck of playing cards that I have been able to find. They started appearing in southern China and in most cases, the cards were similar to the paper money which was used at that time in China. In many cases, the pips would be small coins rather than the hearts, spades, clubs and diamonds we are familiar with today.[9]

Lut Chi cards were typically 1 1/8 x 2 1/4 inches. Lut Chi cards have four suits and superficially some pictures of the suits bear resemblance to the early playing card suits of Asia and later, the European cards.

One style of playing cards illustration had the pips representing the number prominently displayed at the top and bottom of the card with the picture itself being a square at the center of the thin card. This style is called domino cards and these eventually evolved into the game of dominoes.

Early European cards eventually took on the pips we know today: diamonds, hearts, clubs, and spades. One of the most entertaining writings using cards can be found in the story many call *Alice's Adventures in Wonderland* by Charles Lutwidge Dodgson, who most know today as Lewis Carroll. Carroll, an English mathematician, used logic along with literary nonsense to tell his stories. As a side note, in the 1800s, the

---

9    James Masters, "Playing Cards – History and Useful Information," accessed January 23, 2017, http://www.tradgames.org.uk/games/playing-cards.htm.

English called the jack of hearts the knave of hearts and it was this knave that Alice defended in the court of the king of hearts.[10]

So, why is the ace of spades so much different than all the others?

Governments in Europe always put a heavy tax on decks of playing cards in the early years of cards. No one could sell a deck of cards without a tax stamp showing that a tax had been paid on the deck. Taxation was a heavy toll and the main reason that the United States of America fought to free itself from Great Britain.

Card makers decided to put the tax stamp on the ace of spades, the highest-ranking card in the deck. People got used to seeing an ace of spades that was different from all other cards, with a large tax stamp in the middle. In some cases, this ace can be very ornate and artistic.

Later, when tax stamps no longer had to be placed on every deck, card makers continued to make the ace of spades different from the other three aces.

Today, the ace of spades in a deck usually carries the name of the card maker or its trademark.

10    Carroll, Lewis, *Alice's Adventures in Wonderland* (1865).

# CHAPTER EIGHT

## Learn about the Pros

The following biographies are of many of those magicians mentioned in this book as well as a few of the leading magicians of our time who made a successful career with card magic.

# Harry Houdini

Houdini was born on March 24, 1874 and died October 31, 1926. Long before one-name stars like Madonna or Cher, the name Houdini was known everywhere as an excellent entertainer. Houdini, whose birth name was Ehrich Weisz (which was changed to Erich Weiss when he immigrated to America), was a Hungarian con man, magician, escapologist, stunt magician, a skeptic and investigator of spiritualists, a film producer, and an actor. Most of all, he was a brilliant self-promoter.

He might also be one of the most misunderstood magicians of all time. His name has been immortalized and most of this came by his own doing. Growing up with vaudeville, he quickly learned to use the vaudeville style to promote himself in a world where mass communication had yet to be created. People tended to believe what they were told and found it hard, if not impossible, to tell the difference between real news and public relations. To this day, people still believe that Houdini was the greatest magician who ever lived. They cannot be more wrong. What Houdini was greatest at was not performing; he was greatest at promoting. But that's a topic of my next book.

In our modern world of social media, you can still see how the creation of fake news can take hold of the gullible just as the social media did in the days of Houdini. Some things just never seem to change.

# Doug Henning

Doug was born May 3, 1947 in Winnipeg, Manitoba, grew up in Oakville, Ontario, and died February 7, 2000 of liver disease. He was a great magician and one of my close friends.

I first met Doug in the early 1970s when he was a baggage handler for Air Canada working in Toronto, Ontario. There was some magic trick that was for sale and I was trying to buy it. Each time I thought the seller was ready to take my money, I was told that someone else was bidding on it. At first I tried to outbid the other person but it was getting too expensive. I found out that it was Doug who was bidding, so I went to the airport and made a deal with him. We would buy the trick as partners and both of us would share the trick. Doug agreed and we remained friends for the rest of his life.

Doug is credited with reviving the magic show as a form of mass entertainment in North America, beginning in the 1970s. Doug Henning changed the image of the stage magician when he rejected such stereotypical costume accessories as the tuxedo, top hat, thin moustache, goatee, and short hair. He opted instead for long hair, a bushy moustache, and bright and multicolored casual clothes, which gave him a distinctively flamboyant image. Doug's shows used modern rock-and-roll music and was similar to the changing cultures across the world.

Doug Henning had a dream to return magic back to the glory days it had during vaudeville times and earlier. During the height of vaudeville, the top magicians had huge shows with elaborate sets. Shows could easily have up to one hundred cast and crew working a single show.

Doug worked tirelessly and in order to further his career, created a Broadway style show, and managed to receive a grant from the Canadian government to help with the financing. He named the show Spellbound and was joined by fellow Torontonian Ivan Reitman to direct it. Ivan later went on to create some of the most memorial movies including *Ghostbusters* and *Animal House*.

The music was by Howard Shore who went on to create music for many movies including *The Lord of the Rings* and *The Hobbit*.

The show also included actress Jennifer Dale and it was a musical that combined an intense storyline and Doug Henning's magic tricks. The show opened in Toronto and broke box office ticket records in that city.

After catching the attention of New York producers, Doug reworked the show for a larger stage and a larger audience. It was renamed The Magic Show when it went to New York City, with songs composed by Stephen Schwartz who also went on the write the music for Pippin and Wicked. The Magic Show debuted in 1974 and the show ran for four and a half years, earning Doug Henning a Tony Award nomination.

Execs at NBC loved the show and they brought Doug in to discuss a television special. Doug loved the idea of bringing magic to television and when NBC agreed to produce a television special, he was overjoyed. He spent the next eight months reworking his act for television.

Debuting in December 1975, *Doug Henning's World of Magic* captured the attention of more than fifty million viewers. For the following seven years, Doug Henning continued his once-a-year broadcasts, ultimately receiving seven Emmy nominations.

Doug relocated to Los Angeles from Toronto in 1976, where he created his own production company. He would later create stage effects for music videos and concerts performed by musicians such as Earth, Wind & Fire, and Michael Jackson.

One of Doug's greatest strengths was presentation: his natural exuberance and his colorful costumes and props could make very old illusions seem new, and make simple tricks seem like miracles.

# Johnny Carson

He was born John William "Johnny" Carson on October 23, 1925 and died on January 23, 2005. He was an American television host best known for his iconic status as host of *The Tonight Show*.

However, years before his television career, Johnny Carson worked as a stage magician. His interest in magic began when the Carson family moved to Norfolk, Nebraska, where he learned to perform magic tricks at age eight. At age fourteen, he debuted as "The Great Carsoni."[11] Later in life, Carson would often perform magic tricks on his television program and regularly hired magicians to perform on his show.

# Harry Anderson

Harry Anderson, born October 14, 1952 is an Emmy-nominated actor and magician. Born in Newport, Rhode Island, Anderson began his career as a street magician. As an actor, he is most famous for playing the comedic role of Judge Harry Stone on the 1984–1992 television series *Night Court*.[12]

Harry's magic/comedy routine earned him eight appearances on *Saturday Night Live* between 1981 and 1985 and a recurring role as con man "Harry the Hat" on the television show *Cheers*. Harry also toured extensively as a magician and directed the magic/comedy television show *Harry Anderson's Sideshow* in 1987.

Harry made his show unique by dressing in a double-breasted suit and a Stetson style hat, which was why his character on *Cheers* was called Harry the Hat.

---

11    Hopwood, Jon C., "Johnny Carson Mini Bio," accessed January 23, 2017, http://www.imdb.com/name/nm0001992/bio.

12    "Harry Anderson Biography," accessed January 23, 2017, http://www.tcm.com/tcmdb/person/3778%7C0/Harry-Anderson/.

# Criss Angel

Born December 19, 1967, Christopher Nicholas Sarantakos is best known by his stage name Criss Angel. Criss is an American of Greek descent who grew up in Long Island, New York. He was a magician at an early age and likes to be considered an illusionist, musician, escapologist, and stunt magician. He is best known for starring in his own television show, *Criss Angel Mindfreak*.[13]

Criss Angel performed a show called the *World of Illusion* at Madison Square Garden in 1998. Criss then scored a show titled *Criss Angel Mindfreak*, which ran up until January 6, 2003, a run of 600 performances at the World Underground Theater in Times Square. *Criss Angel* was also named International Magicians Society's Magician of the Year in 2001, 2004, 2005, 2007, and 2008.

In 2007, Criss published a book *Mindfreak: Secret Revelations* about magic and his life. The bookbecame a Los Angeles Times bestseller.[5]

# David Blaine

Born David Blaine White on April 4, 1973 in Brooklyn, New York, David Blaine is a world-record-holding magician and endurance artist.[14] He made his name as a magician of street and close-up magic, revolutionizing the way magic is depicted around the world.

On May 19, 1997 Blaine's first television special, *David Blaine: Street Magic*, introduced his unique brand of street magic to the world when it aired on the ABC network. With its strong focus on spectators' reactions and showmanship, Street Magic revolutionized the way magic is

---

13    "Criss Angel Biography," *A&E Television Networks*, last modified May 29, 2014, accessed January 23, 2017, http://www.biography.com/people/criss-angel-244776#magical-persona.

14    "David Blaine Biography," *A&E Television Networks*, last modified December 7, 2015, accessed January 23, 2017, http://www.biography.com/people/david-blaine-12127585#endurance-stunts.

performed and portrayed on television. As Eric Mink wrote in *The New York Daily News*, "Blaine can lay claim to his own brand of wizardry. The magic he offers in tonight's show operates on an uncommonly personal level."[15]

*Street Magic* follows Blaine as he travels the country to entertain unsuspecting people onstreets of New York City, Atlantic City, Dallas, San Francisco, Compton, and the Mojave Desert, recorded by a three-person crew with handheld cameras. Blaine is respected by many magicians for his image, which distinguishes him from other magicians who have performed on television. Jon Racherbaumer, a prolific author, publisher, illustrator, and editor of books and magazines in the field of magic, once commented, "Make no mistake about it, the focus of this show, boys and girls, is not Blaine. It is really about theatrical proxemics; about the show-within-a-show and the spontaneous, visceral reactions of people being astonished."[16]

# Lance Burton

Born William Lance Burton on March 10, 1960, Lance grew up in Louisville, Kentucky. His fascination with magic began when he saw a show by magician Harry Collins during a Christmas party he attended with his mother. Lance was especially intrigued by the trick "The Miser's Dream," in which the magician makes silver dollars appear from thin air and from a spectator's ears. A neighbor gave him a book, *Magic Made Easy*, and Lance quickly learned all ten magic tricks included in the book.[17]

He began performing for other children in the neighborhood, and eventually had his own show in Las Vegas, Nevada for an unprecedented nine years. He has appeared on television many times, including on the

15    Eric Mink, "Magic Special Turns Out To Be Both," *New York Daily News*, May 19, 1997, accessed January 23, 2017, http://www.nydailynews.com/archives/entertainment/magic-special-turns-article-1.753081.

16    "Bingo Bango!" *Magic Directory*, accessed October 6, 2010.

17    "About Lance," *Lance Burton: Master Magician*, accessed January 24, 2017, http://www.lanceburton.com/pages/about-lance.php.

*Jerry Lewis MDA Labor Day Telethon* in 2006 and *The Tonight Show* with both Johnny Carson and Jay Leno. He has also performed in London for Queen Elizabeth and in Washington, D.C. for President Ronald Reagan and his wife.

# Ricky Jay

Born Richard Jay Potash in 1948, Ricky Jay is an American stage magician, actor, historian, and writer. He is considered to be one of the most knowledgeable and skilled sleight-of-hand experts in the United States.[18]

Ricky was born in Brooklyn, New York. As a magician, he has worked extensively with David Mamet, who directed his show *Ricky Jay and His 52 Assistants* at the Second Stage Theatre in New York City.[19] This show earned Ricky the Lucille Lortel and Obie Awards for Outstanding Achievement. Besides New York City, he has also performed in Chicago, Los Angeles, London, and Melbourne, among others.[10]

Ricky's magic background and acting career has led him to roles in the movie *The Prestige* as well as season one of the television show Deadwood as card sharp Eddie Sawyer.[20]

Ricky's card throwing *skills also netted him a listing in the* Guinness Book of World Records for throwing a playing card for distance. Ricky Jay can throw a card 90 miles per hour, reaching a distance of 190 feet. From ten paces, that same card can pierce a watermelon rind.[21]

---

18    "Ricky Jay: the Serious Bio," From the *World Wide Website of Ricky Jay,* accessed January 24, 2017, http://www.rickyjay.com/bio.html.

19    Barbara Hoffman, "Ricky Jay's magical New York," *New York Post,* January 17, 2015, accessed January 24, 2017, http://nypost.com/2015/01/17/ricky-jays-magical-new-york.

20    "Ricky Jay," *IMDb,* accessed January 24, 2017, http://www.imdb.com/name/nm0419633/#actor.

21    Mark Singer, "Secrets of the Magus," *The New Yorker,* April 5, 1993, accessed January 24, 2017, http://www.newyorker.com/magazine/1993/04/05/secrets-of-the-magus.

# Jeff McBride

Also known as Magnus, Jeff McBride was born September 11, 1959. His distinctive magical style was influenced by kabuki, a form of Japanese theater. He was introduced to kabuki at age sixteen while on tour in Japan. After high school, Jeff worked for a time in New York City, eventually becoming a headliner for Caesars Palace's "Magical Empire" in Las Vegas for several years. His magic has been featured on several television shows, including *Criss Angel Mindfreak*.[22]

Jeff founded the McBride Magic and Mystery School in Las VegasVegas, where he seeks to teach stage magic to students of all skill levels and interests.[23] In addition to working with the school, he presents frequently at magic conventions all over the world. He has also taught for members of The Smithsonian, the International Brotherhood of Magicians, and other groups.

# The Pendragons

Jonathan and Charlotte Pendragon were an award-winning husband-and-wife team known for their illusion magic. The duo first met in the 1970s while studying at the University of California, Irvine. At the time, Jonathan was studying drama while Charlotte pursued dance. Both worked as stunt doubles for films. After the couple began dating, they started performing magic together. Their physical illusions earned them the title Best Illusionists in the 1990 International Magic Awards.[24]

22   "About Jeff McBride," *McBride Magic*, accessed January 24, 2017, http://www.mcbridemagic.com/pages/about.php.

23   "Welcome to the Magic & Mystery School," *Jeff McBride's Magic & Mystery School*, accessed January 24, 2017, http://www.magicalwisdom.com/about/welcome.

24   Mark Chalon Smith, "Pendragons Escape With 'Best Illusionists' Award: Magic: The couple are elated that judges chose them over David Copperfield," *Los Angeles Times*, November 2, 1990, accessed January 25, 2017, http://

Jonathan Pendragon referred to their unique style as "Physical Grand Illusion," where the tricks focused more on physical performance than props. He invented several famous illusions, including Clearly Impossible, where a woman appears to be sawed in half.[25]

The talented team split up in 2009, after decades of joint performances.[26]

# Penn & Teller

For Penn Jillette and Raymond Teller, comedy and illusion go hand-in-hand. Their act is one of the longest running headliner shows in Las Vegas, and they've won the "Las Vegas Magicians of the Year" award eight times. Their career has also taken them to Broadway and on tour around the world.[27]

Cur*rently, they play the hosts in the television show* Penn & Teller: Fool Us! where new magicians are given an opportunity to show off their stuff. They've also written several best-selling books.

# Val Valentino

Born Leonard Monatono in June 14, 1956 in Los Angeles, the magician Val Valentino gained notoriety by starring in four magic specials on the Fox Network. He goes by the stage name the Masked Magician or Mr. M.[28]

articles.latimes.com/1990-11-02/entertainment/ca-3929_1_david-copperfield.

25    "About," *Jonathan Pendragon: Master of Imagination*, accessed January 25, 2017, http://www.jonathanpendragon.com.

26    "Jonathan Pendragon," *IMDb*, accessed January 25, 2017, http://www.imdb.com/name/nm0946396/bio?ref_=nm_ov_bio_sm#mini_bio.

27    "Bio," *Penn & Teller*, accessed January 25, 2017, http://www.pennandteller.com/wordpress/gallery/bio-2.

28    Dayanara S. Ryelle, "Val Valentino Biography," *IMDb*, accessed January 25, 2017, http://www.imdb.com/name/nm0884349/bio.

Val entered the magic world at a young age. When he was five years old, his father gave him a trick called "the ball vase."[20] This is a simple effect where a ball is placed on the top of a small vase. The magician covers the top of the vase while secretly pocketing the ball, then reveals the now-empty vase. Finally, the vase is covered again and uncovered to reveal that the ball is back on the top of the vase.

Before starring in Fox's show *Breaking the Magicians' Code: Magic's Biggest Secrets Finally Revealed*, Val had spent years performing in Las Vegas. After taking on the persona of the Masked Magician for the show, he retired after two years.[20]

Many magicians feel that Valentino crossed the line by revealing how magicians perform most of the classic tricks of the modern time.

# Dai Vernon

Dai Vernon (pronounced as DIE) was a close personal friend of mine. Born on June 11, 1894 and died on August 21, 1992, he was commonly known as the Professor, and was a Canadian magician, although he was known worldwide for his magic abilities.

He was the greatest living expert on sleight of hand, and many of the tricks in this book can be traced back to his performances, proving that if you work hard and learn the tricks in this book you will be performing tricks that were also performed by the very best magician in the craft.

# Walter Gibson

As mentioned earlier in this book, Walter Gibson was a close friend, a great magician, an author of magic books, and the creator of the book and radio series *The Shadow*.[29]

29     Wolfgang Saxon, "Walter B. Gibson, Creator of 'The Shadow,' Dead at 88," *The New York Times*, December 7, 1985, accessed January 26, 2017, http://

Among his huge body of work, one book in particular is *The Complete Illustrated Book of Card Magic*, which was published by Doubleday in 1969 and is a glorious book of card magic. I considered it my card trick bible when I was a professional entertainer. Although this book is out of print and hard to find, it is well worth the search.

In his day, many magical performers did not appreciate that his books revealed how tricks worked. His opinion and mine is that the knowledge of the trick is less important than the performance of the trick.

As the world's leading authority on everything magical, Walter cared little about what other magicians thought and more about the advancement of the art of magic as a whole. All of his works are well worth reading and his words on performance and the handling of magic are as true today as they were fifty years ago.

---

www.nytimes.com/1985/12/07/arts/walter-b-gibson-the-creator-of-the-shadow-deat-at-88.html.

# CHAPTER NINE
## Books on Card Tricks

There is a wealth of magic to be learned in the thousands of books written on the subject of magic, if you pardon my pun. The following titles are great books, and I have learned a great deal from them myself over the years. Let this be a guide, either a starting point for new magicians or a resource for the more experienced. No matter where you are on your journey of prestidigitation, these titles will not disappoint you.

*Super Little Giant Book of Card Tricks* by Diagram Visual (Paperback - Nov 1, 2007)

*The Complete Illustrated Book of Card Magic* by Walter Gibson Doubleday (Hardcover 1969)

*Giant Book of Card Tricks* by Bob Longe and Inc. Sterling Publishing Co. (Paperback - Jul 1, 2003)

*Encyclopedia of Card Tricks* by Jean Hugard and John J., Jr. Crimmins (Paperback - Jan 2003)

*World's Best Card Tricks* by Bob Longe (Paperback - Jun 30, 1992)

*Easy-to-Do Card Tricks for Children (Become a Magician)* by Karl Fulves (Paperback - Dec 1, 1989) - Illustrated

*Card Tricks for Beginners (Dover Books on Magic)* by Wilfrid Jonson (Paperback - Feb 2, 2004)

*Scarne on Card Tricks* by John Scarne (Paperback - Mar 10, 2003) - Illustrated

*The Ultimate Book of Card & Magic Tricks* by Bob Longe (Paperback - Aug 28, 2006)

*Self-Working Card Tricks (Cards, Coins, and Other Magic)* by Karl Fulves (Paperback - Jun 1, 1976) - Illustrated

*Young Magician: Card Tricks (Young Magician (Sterling)* by Oliver Ho and David Garbot (Paperback - Aug 1, 2005)

*The Amazing Magical Wonder Deck: A Box of Illusions with Trick Cards and Instruction Book* by Mr. Mysterio (Cards - Nov 10, 2005)

*A Little Giant Book: Tricks & Pranks (Little Giant Books)* by E. Richard Churchill (Paperback - Aug 1, 2007)

*Mark Wilson's Little Book Of Card Tricks (Miniature Editions)* by Mark Wilson (Hardcover - Nov 1, 2000) - Illustrated

*The Ultimate Card Trick Book* by Eve Devereux (Paperback - 2002)

*The Amazing Book of Magic & Card Tricks* by Jon Tremaine (Hardcover - Aug 1998)

*The Ultimate Card Trick Book: Master the Magic of over 70 Amazing Tricks* by Eve Devereux (Hardcover - Dec 1994)

*The Everything Card Tricks Book: Over 100 Amazing Tricks to Impress Your Friends And Family! (Everything: Sports and Hobbies)* by Dennis Rourke (Paperback - Sep 1, 2005)

*Card Tricks (An Easy-Read Activity Book)* by Ken Reisberg, Arline Oberman, and Marvin Oberman (School & Library Binding - Aug 1980)

*Clever Card Tricks Book & Kit* by Bob Longe (Hardcover - Mar 28, 2006)

*The Little Giant Book of Card Tricks* by Bob Longe (Paperback - Jun 30, 2000)

*The Jumbo Book of Card Tricks & Games* by Bob Longe (Paperback - Dec 31, 2001)

# THE NEXT TO FINAL WORD

Many of the greatest illusions from before 1940 would cause little or no interest in today's world of technology. Few would be impressed with a robot that can deal cards or a buzz saw that could cut a person in two. It has been done, and overdone. True enough, many tricks of days ago can be updated and retuned in order to seek greatness, but unfortunately, there are too few magicians who are skilled enough to perform the tricks, too few venues to house or host the shows, and too much competition for entertainment in general today.

Card magic, on the other hand, endures the test of time. Cards have not changed in overall appearance or use over the past two hundred years. Most people have played card games in their lifetime and are familiar with all fifty-two cards and the two jokers. That is what makes them such a great magic tool. They are familiar to all.

Looking back on the world of magic as it relates to cards, it is hard to imagine a magician not being able to reach into his bag of tricks and say the world's most famous magic line, "Pick a card."

I hope you enjoyed this book, because I certainly did enjoy writing it.

Herbert L. Becker

# THE ROAD TO SUCCESS

"How do you get to Carnegie Hall?" the guy asked his cab driver. The reply, "Practice. Practice. Practice." This might be a corny old joke, but the truth seems to be there. If you want to be good at something, anything, give it all the practice you can.

Author Malcolm Gladwell wrote a book called *Outliers*. He said about his book, "'Outlier' is a scientific term to describe things or phenomena that lie outside normal experience. In the summer, in Paris, we expect most days to be somewhere between warm and very hot. But imagine if you had a day in the middle of August where the temperature fell below freezing. That day would be outlier. And while we have a very good understanding of why summer days in Paris are warm or hot, we know a good deal less about why a summer day in Paris might be freezing cold. In this book, I'm interested in people who are outliers—in men and women who, for one reason or another, are so accomplished and so extraordinary and so outside of ordinary experience that they are as puzzling to the rest of us as a cold day in August."

One of the chapters of *Outliers* talks about the importance of practice. Studies suggest that the key to success in any field has nothing to do with talent. It's simply practice, 10,000 hours of it—twenty hours a week for ten years. Gladwell calls it the 10,000 Hour Rule.

"It takes ten years of extensive training to excel in anything," Herbert Simon - Nobel Laureate.[30]

---

30    Balyi, Istvan, PhD, and Ann Hamilton, MPE. "Long-term Athlete Development: Trainability in Childhood and Adolescence." Olympic Coach, 2004, 4.

Doug Henning is credited with reviving the magic show as a form of mass entertainment in North America, beginning in the 1970s. Henning changed the image of the stage magician when he rejected such stereotypical costume accessories as the tuxedo, top hat, thin moustache, goatee, and short hair. He opted instead for long hair, a bushy moustache, and bright-multicolored casual clothes, which gave him a distinctively flamboyant image. Some considered him an overnight sensation, but let's take a closer look at how he became an overnight sensation.

Henning performed his first show at the age of fourteen at the birthday party of a friend. He was inspired by his audience's spellbound reaction. Within a few months of placing an ad in a local newspaper, he launched a series of performances on local television in Toronto, and as an entertainer at parties. He opened his first major show at age twenty-six, twelve years after he debuted as a magician. By his own account, he had already logged more than 5,000 hours of rehearsal time before opening his initial run on the bigger stages in Toronto.

Doug took his magic to Broadway, opening on May 28, 1974 and closing on Dec 31, 1978 for a total of 1,920 performances. Before that he performed with a show called *Spellbound* in Toronto, which after eight months of rehearsal, a last-minute show cancellation allowed them to open at the Royal Alexandra Theatre for a total of thirty shows.

In all, the math is simple: 1,950 shows over a period of five and a half years with a total of 4,875 hours of practice between the age of fourteen and twenty-six. Add to that 4,875 hours of performance time on Broadway and on stage in Toronto, not to mention 125 hours of rehearsal during the eight months leading up to his first big show for a total of, you guessed it, 10,000 hours.

It was not until he clocked his full 10,000 hours following his Broadway success that NBC approached Henning about producing a television special. He spent the next eight months reworking and rehearsing his act for television. Debuting in December 1975, Doug Henning's *World of Magic* captured the attention of more than fifty million viewers. For the following seven years, Doug Henning continued his once-a-year broadcasts, ultimately earning seven Emmy nominations.

So you can see, Henning's great success did not happen "overnight." It happened after more than 10,000 hours were logged.

As most magic books will teach you, this one included, practice your magic in front of a mirror. This should be considered preliminary practice. In front of the mirror is the practice to ensure that others cannot see the secret or deceptive moves. The 10,000-hour rule of practice, which we are discussing here, is the practice of your act in front of a real live audience.

The timing of the trick, the words you say, the combination of tricks you perform, and the length of time you perform is what you are practicing. Which tricks work, when they work, and on whom they work.

Tricks that might impress children might not do a thing for adults and tricks that will leave a teenager open-mouthed and in awe might go right over the head of a ten-year-old.

In order to succeed, you must practice, experiment, and study your performance as well as how your audience receives it.

Early in this book, I mentioned the fact that a magician might only know about eight tricks, which might be all you need for the average performance. However, it might be one set of eight tricks for children under ten, another set for teenagers, and a third set for adults. There might be a trick that works on all ages, but you will never know until you take the time to practice your craft in front of an audience.

Doug Henning used to say, "The difficult must become easy. Easy must become habit. And habit must become beautiful."

After 10,000 hours of performing the tricks, you will find that they become part of your habit and they will fit into your comfort level.

Many magicians begin their craft as children, perhaps beginning to perform when they are between eight and ten years of age. If they continue to work on their craft during their teenage years, they will have performed for many hours in front of a wide range of people. To me, what seems to be a mistake with magicians is the thought that bigger and better tricks are needed to become more successful or famous. In truth, you simply need to be proficient at the tricks you do have in order to reach a higher level of success. From within these pages you can easily create several acts, which, if practiced and performed enough, can easily move you into the ranks of the professional magician. It won't happen overnight unless you can put in the 10,000 hours you need overnight.

As neurologist Daniel Levitin says:

In study after study, of composers, basketball players, fiction writers, ice-skaters, concert pianists, chess players, master criminals, this number comes up again and again. Ten thousand hours is equivalent to roughly three hours a day, or 20 hours a week, of practice over 10 years. No one has yet found a case in which true world-class expertise was accomplished in less time. It seems that it takes the brain this long to assimilate all that it needs to know to achieve true mastery.[31]

10,000 hours might sound like a long time but just look at the success rate; some of the most successful people in the world have shown that it was the practice of 10,000 hours which gave them the edge they needed for greatness. People such as Bill Gates, the Beatles, Steve Jobs, Doug Henning, and Mozart all needed this edge, regardless of any talent they might have been born with.

The formulation of the 10,000-hour rule seems to have been derived from a study done by Dr. Ericsson and colleagues that was published in the Psychological Review in 1993. They looked at the accomplished violinists of Berlin's Academy of Music, who had been divided into three groups: stars, solid magicians, and those who could teach but not make it big. What they found was the amount of practice at each level of quality differed, and it was those stars that had by age twenty, practiced about 10,000 hours.[32]

According to Dr. Ericsson's current statements, the details of this so-called rule are much more complex. He has further defined it in his research specifically, that practice has to be focused, driven, and useful. Doing something complacently for ten years does not actually make you an expert.

In an update to the excerpt of his article, Dr. Ericsson says:

> For example, the critical difference between expert musicians differing in the level of attained solo performance concerned the amounts of time they had spent in solitary practice during their music development, which totaled around 10,000 hours by age twenty for the

31    Delamontagne, Robert P. *The Retiring Mind: How to Make the Psychological Transition to Retirement.* Fairview Imprints, 2010, 40.

32    Ericsson, K. Anders, Ralf Th. Krampe, and Clemens Tesch-Romer, "The Role of Deliberate Practice in the Acquisition of Expert Performance," *Psychological Review* vol. 100 no. 3 (1993): 363-406, http://projects.ict.usc.edu/itw/gel/EricssonDeliberatePracticePR93.PDF.

best experts, around 5,000 hours for the least accomplished expert musicians and only 2,000 hours for serious amateur pianists. More generally, the accumulated amount of deliberate practice is closely related to the attained level of performance of many types of experts, such as musicians, chess players and athletes.[33]

I have discovered that often, the secret of a trick is far less interesting or exciting than watching the trick being performed. It is the wonderment of the process happening before your eyes, which is exciting, whereas the secret itself can and might seem mundane, simple, and superfluous.

Is there any value to disclosing how you accomplished the trick? This is solely dependent upon your goals and your audience. Certainly, you will not be surprised when you are asked to perform the trick again or asked, "how did you do it?"

Between the magician and the audience, there are many rituals taking place. The audience wants to enjoy the trick, they want to figure out the trick, and they might want to mess up the trick in order to make it not work. The magician knows all these aspects and he is trying to fool the audience, put them off guard and keep them in suspense. Each party has their own agenda and that is what makes it so much fun.

With the right amount of practice, the magician will be able to achieve his goals and along the way, create a little bit of illusion, enjoyment, and fun for himself and those who are watching.

It is my desire that this book will be an inspiration to those who read it and those who benefit from the enjoyment from it, either as a performer or as a spectator of a performance.

Magic tricks have captivated audiences for as long as man has been walking on this earth and I see no reason for that to end anytime soon. A few tricks up your sleeve will always come in handy.

Remember what the cabbie said, the way to get to Carnegie Hall is to practice, practice, practice.

Herbert L. Becker
December 2016

---

33    Ericsson, K. Anders, Ralf Th. Krampe, and Clemens Tesch-Romer, "Expert performance and deliberate practice: An updated excerpt from Ericsson," Florida State University, 2000, https://psy.fsu.edu/faculty/ericssonk/ericsson.exp.perf.html.

# GLOSSARY

| | |
|---|---|
| Cut | To divide the deck and then place the top half below the bottom half. |
| Double flip | A performing skill in which the magician makes his audience believe they're seeing the top card of a deck, when in fact the magician has flipped over the top two cards. |
| Fan | To spread out a deck of cards, allowing a spectator to pick one. |
| Force | A performing skill in which the magician controls which card a spectator picks. |
| Jog | Move the card toward a person without removing from deck. |
| Locator card | A specially prepared card that helps the magician find a spectator's card in the deck. |
| Patter | Another word for "talk." Stage patter can be an important skill in performing magic. |
| Pip | A term for the suit symbol on each card: clubs, spades, diamonds, or hearts. |
| Riffle | A one-handed bridge shuffle. |
| Square | To straighten the cards in a deck. |

# ABOUT THE AUTHOR

**Herbert L. Becker** was voted Best USA Magician in 1975 and 1976 by *Houdini Magic Magazine*. His previous books, *All the Secrets of Magic Revealed* (1997) and *101 Greatest Magic Secrets* (2002) have sold over 300,000 copies in thirteen languages and were turned into a series of television programs for Fox Television. He helped open the first Guinness museum, toured with Guinness on Parade, and performed at the Steel Pier and Radio City Music Hall with the Guinness Show.

Scan to visit

http://magicweb.com/